The Collector's Encyclopedia of

R. S. PRUSSIA

The Collector's Encyclopedia of

R. S. PRUSSIA
and other
R. S. and E. S. Porcelain

by
Mary Frank Gaston

COLLECTOR BOOKS

Additional copies of this book may be ordered from:

COLLECTOR BOOKS
P.O. Box 3009
Paducah, Kentucky 42001
or
The author: Mary Frank Gaston
P.O. Box 342
Bryan Texas 77806

$24.95 plus $1.00 for postage and handling

COPYRIGHT: Mary Frank Gaston, 1982
ISBN: 0-89145-178-1

Design and Photography by Jerry Gaston

Printed by Taylor Publishing Company, Dallas, Texas.

To Jerry and Jeremy

Acknowledgements

The completion of this book on R. S. Prussia was made possible because of the help of many individuals. I express my deepest appreciation to —

Jerry Gaston, my husband and never failing base of encouragement and enthusiasm. He traveled with me across the United States to photograph personally all the beautiful pictures for this book. He was also responsible for the editing and design of the book.

Professor Lon Shelby, Southern Illinois University, for obtaining archival information in Germany, and Professor Donald Detwiler, Southern Illinois University, for providing vauable historical information.

Jeremy Gaston, my ten year old son, for his understanding when I was busy with "Prussia," and for his help when needed.

And Vera and Frank Ballow, my parents, for taking care of Jeremy while we were away from home on so many occasions.

"Prussia" collectors and dealers are among the warmest and most cordial people I have ever met. For their generous hospitality and cooperation in allowing us to photograph their beautiful porcelain and for sharing their views, thoughts, and insights on the subject of "R. S.," I extend a very special THANK YOU to —

Mr. and Mrs. James Baxter, Mt. Vernon, Illinois
Mr. and Mrs. Bob Feely, Barby Sales, Emmaus, Pennsylvania
Mrs. Marian L. Fine, Alburquerque, New Mexico
Jessie Hall, Jessie's Showcase of Antiques, Fort Worth, Texas
Mr. and Mrs. Ray Hoeppner, New Albany, Indiana
Imogene Meissner, Imo's Folly, Granbury, Texas
Mr. and Mrs. James Sights, House of R. S., Robards, Kentucky
   and to —
Allen Antiques
Phil Anderson, Anderson's Antiques & Art Gallery, Oklahoma City, Oklahoma

Anna Belle's Antiques, Oklahoma City, Oklahoma
Joe Bell, Black Gold Antiques, Oklahoma City, Oklahoma
Hazel Boggs
Joe and Dolores Broaddus, J & D Antiques, Moro, Illinois
Glen and Glenda Cooley, Tommorrow's Treasures, Oklahoma City, Oklahoma
Kathleen and Jack Cunningham, Pot Luck Antiques, Texarkana, Texas
Tom Foster, Tom's Antiques, Tulsa, Okalhoma
Marian Gilbert, Decatur, Georgia
Doris and Harold Hagen, Antique Nook, Las Vegas, Nevada
Berkley Hunt
Oren and Donna McCaslin, Hogeye Antiques, Phillipsburg, Missouri
C. R. and Billie McChesnee, Pine Cone Antiques, Arp, Texas
Ray and Jean Ludwig, Henderson House Antiques, Henderson, Texas
Mannan's Antiques, Indianapolis, Indiana
Martini's, Las Vegas, Nevada
Mary's Den of Antiquity, Las Vegas, Nevada
Laura Lou Medley, Laura's Antiques & Gifts, Oklahoma City, Oklahoma
Norm Miller, The Shop Antiques, Salina, Kansas
Trudy Miller, Dallas, Texas
Old Coffee Mill Antiques, Carthage, Missouri
Olde Towne Antique Mall, Springfield, Missouri
Jeane Parris, Sugarplums, etc., Las Vegas, Nevada
Riggs Antiques, Evansville, Indiana
Ken Roberts, Ken's Antiques, Tulsa, Oklahoma
Marge Shellabarger, Shellabarger's Antiques, Sullivan, Illinois
The Yester-Year Mart, Las Vegas, Nevada
Edward A. Wheeler, Mt. Vernon, Illinois
Additional thanks to Mr. and Mrs. James Sights for items featured on the cover.

Preface

All that's "gold" does not glitter might be an appropriate description of one of the most active fields of antiques collecting today. R. S. Prussia porcelain has been collected avidly in this country since the early 1960's, and the pace has increased during the last few years. Today, pieces of Prussia command top dollar throughout the nation. In addition, the porcelain products manufactured by the same family, Erdmann and Reinhold Schlegelmilch, but whose marks use E. S. or R. S. intials with other symbols, are also currently in demand, and are expected to be more in demand in the future.

I talked to antique dealers and R. S. Prussia collectors about their ideas for a basic book on the subject. They reported that there were several things about Prussia which had not been dealt with extensively or had been neglected. They encouraged me to provide a book with the widest possible scope.

First, there is the question of price. General price guides often include a small section on R. S. Prussia and other R. S. Marks. Collectors and dealers inform me though that often these prices are not accurate. With the rapidly increasing prices each year, some of the quoted prices do not reflect the actual cost of an object today. While I know that price guides are sometimes controversial, I have compiled a current price range based on prices the pictured items in this book were bringing during the summer and fall of 1981. (Please refer to the separate *Price Guide* for further comments on the price information.) Also, there was a consensus that the emphasis should be on the types of R. S. Prussia that are still available rather than concentrating on the more rare and exotic pieces. Thus, the majority of pieces pictured in this book were obtained from antique shops and show exhibits across the country rather than personal collections.

Second, unmarked Prussia is an area of concern to many dealers as well as collectors. This subject needed investigation, and I have tried to deal with the problem head on, hoping that my comments will prove helpful.

Third, R. S. Prussia is virtually unique in the numerous elaborate and artistic shapes or molds of the pieces. Generally, porcelain of the late 19th century is collected for the beauty of its decoration. Most of the porcelain objects from that period in history are relatively simple in form, because porcelain was primarily a medium for decoration. Numerous examples of R. S. Prussia porcelain, however, have very complex shapes. If the pieces had been undecorated (that is, left as "blanks,") their shape alone would merit artistic appreciation. At first glance, to attempt to identify the various molds seems to be an impossible task. A mold identification system, however, will make it relatively easy to describe a piece (especially when either a buyer or seller cannot see the piece in person or in a photograph.) Thus, for the first time, an R. S. Prussia Mold Identification System is presented. It includes unmarked as well as marked pieces. My mold identification will be expanded as I identify and photograph other molds for future study.

Some other topics that must be included in a reference source are, of course, information about the marks and general history of each company. In fact the most troublesome task connected with this book results from the fact that so few facts are available. Companies usually do not forsee being the topic of future historical interest, so records that would clarify and ease the job are often not maintained, or are destroyed through time. With the Schlegelmilchs' factories located in Germany during both World Wars, it is easy to see how little historical information, even if kept, would still exist.

As I am somewhat a thwarted detective, however, I decided to try to find out or work out a plausible chronology of factory markings. My efforts were not completely successful, but I think the chronology presented and the reasons for it can help both new and experienced collectors when faced with the many marks attributed to the Schlegelmilchs. I am aware, of course, that some people argue that marks do not mean everything; but for most people marks are important. People would not frequently look at the mark as the first thing when examining a piece, if that were not true. So instead of just saying here are the marks used by the Schlegelmilchs, I have extended my efforts not only to present the marks, but to suggest their chronology.

The scope of this book also is not limited to R. S. Prussia. Although R. S. Prussia is the primary topic, I have included E. S. and other R. S. marks. These marks are discussed with a possible chronology suggested as well. Color photographs and current prices for pieces with these marks are also presented. (Please note that because of relatively few items on the market with Oscar Schlegelmilch's marks, information concerning his company is not included.)

Several problems confront R. S. Prussia collectors and dealers. One problem is unmarked examples, but reproductions, fake marks, misleading marks, altered and repaired items, double marks, mold marks, and other "Prussia" marks are also areas of confusion and concern. These problems are discussed in detail. Photographs of R. S. Prussia-type new items, misleading marks, and the fake mark are illustrated.

Color photographs of the Schlegelmilch porcelains are an important feature of this book. Hopefully, you will enjoy identifying your special pieces of Schlegelmilch porcelain presented, realizing of course, that numerous examples still are "out there" to be illustrated and documented. If you do not find your "piece" in this book, we trust you will in later editions. Readers having examples of *Molds* not included here are cordially invited to write me at P.O. Box 342, Bryan, Texas, 77806 so that they might be included in future editions.

Mary Frank Gaston
September 1981

Contents

1.
What is R. S. Prussia?

R. S. PRUSSIA is a type of 19th to 20th century porcelain found in decorative objects and table wares. These objects are back stamped with a distinguishing trademark composed of the initials R. S. inside a wreath with a star above and the word Prussia underneath (see Section 2 and Plates 4 to 11). Objects with this mark were manfactured during the last quarter of the 19th century and through the first years of the 20th century by two brothers, Erdmann and Reinhold Schlegelmilch, in the Germanic area in Europe known until the end of World War I as Prussia. For a better understanding of the history of their porcelain, and to verify the period when it was produced, it is necessary to know some basic facts about porcelain in general, the history of the area where the factories were located, and world conditions during the time of the companies.

R. S. Prussia is a type of porcelain although pieces are often referred to just as china. But all items called china are not necessarily porcelain. Porcelain is a type of pottery, and pottery is an object made from clay. Pottery is either earthenware or stoneware, and porcelain technically is a form of stoneware. Although porcelain and stoneware have some common characteristics, they differ in one important respect: porcelain is translucent (light can pass through), but stoneware is opaque (light is blocked). Thus for clarity and differentiation, porcelain is often considered as a third type of pottery.

While earthenware and stoneware can be made from many different types of earth, porcelain is made from a specific type of earth, kaolin, found only in certain areas of the world. Kaolin is composed of hydrated aluminum silicates, and accounts for at least 50% of the formula for porcelain. Feldspar and quartz are the other ingredients. Porcelain manufactured from kaolin, feldspar, and quartz is called true or natural porcelain as these ingredients are found naturally in the earth. *Hard paste* is also a term frequently used for true porcelain, the Schlegelmilchs' porcelain being an example. Hard paste porcelain differs from soft paste porcelain and bone paste porcelain (bone china), because their chief ingredients do not exist naturally. Bone ash from the calcined bones of animals is the chief ingredient for bone paste, and glass or glass like materials made up a large percentage of the mixture for the artificial soft paste porcelain made during the seventeenth century. (For more detail in the types and processes of porcelain manufacturing, see pages 10 to 13 of Mary Frank Gaston, *The Collector's Encyclopedia of Limoges Porcelain,* published by Collector Books.)

Porcelain was discovered and manufactured by the Chinese many centuries ago. The name porcelain comes from the Portuguese word, *porcella,* the shell made by the cowrie, a type of mollusk. This shell was translucent and resembled the wares that the Portuguese were importing from China during the 1500s. The enthusiasm for porcelain objects spread quickly across Europe. Leaders of many countries wanted examples of this new art form and began importing it for their own use. Soon several countries set up trading or importing companies in the Orient in order to supply the European demand. Naturally, when anything becomes so popular, attempts are made locally to copy or duplicate it. Although there were many attempts throughout the years, success in manufacturing the true, or hard paste, porcelain of China was not accomplished in Europe until circa 1708. The person credited with this discovery was Johann Fredrich Böttger, an alchemist of Meissen (Germany). His work led to the formation of the Royal Meissen Porcelain Company which is noted as the first true porcelain company in the western world. The Meissen Company was able to keep its formula secret for some time, but through the years, as workers left the factory, they took the knowledge of the process with them. Eventually other centers in Europe as well as other German areas were able to implement this type of production. Also, other Europeans were independently making the same discovery as Böttger. Thus, by the end of the 1700s, hard paste procelain production was not confined to the Meissen Company.

Meissen was located in an area of central Europe that was composed of Teutonic or Germanic speaking peoples. At the time of the discovery of procelain by Böttger, Germany did not exist as a nation. There were many independent or sovereign areas whose boundaries were in an almost constant state of change due to wars and treaties. In the area around Meissen, other Germanic states set up porcelain compaines under royal patronage during the middle 1700s. In the 1800s, the porcelain industry developed in the private sector, however, and royalty no longer had a monopoly on the industry. As a result of the beginning of private ownership of factories, we have R. S. Prussia porcelain.

The year 1861 is the recorded founding date of Erdmann Schlegelmilch's procelain factory in Suhl, a town located in a region called Thuringia. This Germanic area was once part of the state of Saxony, but this particular part of Saxony was conquered by another Germanic state, Prussia, circa 1815. The Thuringia area was rich in deposits of the necessary ingredients for hard paste procelain. Many factories were established by individuals in this region during the 1800s. Some years later, circa 1869, Erdmann's brother, Reinhold began manufacturing porcelain in Tillowitz, a town in Upper Silesia. This part of Silesia was also under Prussian domination. Prussia was in fact the largest of the Germanic states. In 1871, a consolidation of the Germanic independent areas, including Prussia, was finally achieved with the formation of the

Second German Empire (there had been earlier attempts at consolidation). This empire endured until the end of World War I.

Both areas where the Schlegelmilch brothers started their factories were rich in the natural ingredients for true porcelain. Their factories were started at a time when there was a large demand for porcelain items by common people, not just royalty. Most importantly, American and Canadian markets provided a huge market for such wares during the last part of the 19th century. Statistics show that the Schlegelmilchs were just one of many who took advantage of this unique opportunity in the history of porcelain. Approximately 600 pottery and procelain companies with approximately 17,000 workers were operating in the German states in 1850. In the latter part of the 1800s, a large export business developed between Germany and the United States and Canada. The people of North America were anxious to purchase true porcelain chiefly for the advantages of porcelain over earthenware: namely translucency and vitreosity. This latter quality is very important. Vitreosity means glass-like. This quality is achieved when a glaze, similar in ingredients to those used for the body of an object, is applied to an object after it has been fired (baked) at a high temperture, around 900 degress centigrade. When the vitreous glaze is applied the object is fired again at even higher tempertures, from 1400 to 1600 degrees centigrade. During this firing, the glaze and the body of the object actually fuse together. The glaze cannot be penetrated. Thus crazing does not occur to hard paste vitreous objects. Anything that comes into contact with such pieces can be washed off. Items will not become discolored if something with a staining quality comes into contact with the piece. Prior to the large scale exporting of true porcelain to the United States from Europe in the late 1800s, earthenwares were the main type of pottery available, with most of those coming from England.

Industrialization and cheap labor in the German factories combined to make the porcelain products available in large supply and at a reasonable cost to a large section of the American and Canadian public. As a result, small concerns, such as the Schlegelmichs' were allowed to prosper. The companies which manufactured porcelain chiefly for export are not discussed in much detail by German historians and antiquarians of pottery and porcelain for several reasons. First, the majority of the products of these companies was shipped out of the country, so there are relatively few examples found locally. Second, the age of this porcelain does not qualify for "antique" status among European or German collectors. Third, the types of pieces manufactured, chiefly table wares and decorative accessories, were decorated with transfer designs and mass produced for little cost. They do not qualify for works of art which were hand molded, hand decorated, and one of a kind objects which are found in museums. As a result very little historical information exists concerning the Schlegelmilch companies.

It appears that the factories of both Schlegelmilch brothers marked their products for a time with the RSP trademark. Some European reference sources, however, attribute the mark only to Erdmann's factory at Suhl. But examples are seen which not only have the RSP mark but also "Reinhold Schlegelmilch, Tillowitz, Germany." (See Plates 7 and 8, also 9.) Thus one cannot say conclusively that a particular piece came from the Suhl or the Tillowitz factory unless it specifically has an identifying name in addition to the R. S. Prussia mark. Because the identifying initials "R. S." are the same as Reinhold Schlegelmilch, it is understandable that pieces marked R. S. Prussia are frequently attributed only to his factory at Tillowitz, but in fact these initials actually refer to the brothers' father, Rudolph Schlegelmilch, according to Clifford J. Schlegelmilch in his *Handbook of Erdmann and Reinhold Schlegelmilch—Prussia—Germany and Oscar Schlegelmilch—Germany.*

The peak years of importing fancy porcelain in America were during the mid 1870s through the early 1900s. The life style of the United States not only was quite elegant at the upper social levels, but it was also much more detailed and complex at the middle levels than is the case today. A variety of table and dresser accessories as well as *objects d'art* were considered necessary for the genteel life styles of that era.

Not only the types of pieces but also the decorative styles of the porcelain products give a clue to the time of manufacture of the wares. Changing art forms and world conditions from the turn of the century through its first quarter had quite an impact not only on the styles and types of porcelain manufactured by the Schlegelmilch brothers, but on their business in general. (Please refer to Section 2 and Section 3 for a discussion of these later years.)

2.
Distinguishing Characteristics of R. S. Prussia Porcelain

KNOWING WHAT R. S. Prussia porcelain is and its place in history, what makes the porcelain so appealing to collectors? What are its outstanding features? Perhaps the most outstanding characteristic is its variation. Few other porcelain companies of the same period manufactured so vast an array of items in so many different shapes and sizes with as many different themes and finishes of decoration. These features present an overall "image" of R. S. Prussia. Most Prussia is ornatley fashioned and richly decorated. Of course there are exceptions—simply shaped objects plainly decorated, but these are more the exception than the rule. The distinguishing characteristics of R. S. Prussia porcelain can be categorized as (1) Marks; (2) Types of Objects; (3) Shapes; (4) Decoration Methods; (5) Decoration Themes; (6)Color Backgrounds; and (7) Finishes. I shall describe these characteristics and relative identifying terms in this section so that the captions to the photographs can be brief, concise, and easy to read.

R. S. Prussia Marks

The mark on the back of R. S. Prussia Porcelain (RSP) is composed of a green wreath with rust-red edges, a red star at the top, and red lettering of the initials R. S. (inside the wreath), and Prussia (with a period) beneath the wreath. (See Plate 4). This mark is often accompanied with Reinhold Schlegelmilch's marks (see Plates 8 and 9). The mark varies in size from very small to quite large. Collectors refer to the mark as the RED MARK. The same mark can be green, however (see Plates 5 and 7), or the shades of red can vary. This color differentiation was probably caused by the firing procedures after the mark was placed on the object. It is also possible that just one of the factories used the green mark. Examples with the green mark or marks with varying shades of red are not frequently seen in comparison to pieces with the Red Mark. Sometimes pieces with these other colored marks are not as ornate or decorative as those having the red mark, but it cannot be proved that these are "fake" marks as is sometimes suggested. (Reproductions, and questionable marks, are discussed in Section 4 on Collector's Problems.)

Most RSP marks appear to have been applied after the second firing of the procelain which produced the vitreous glaze. As a result the marks are not "sealed." Although the mark would have been fired again after it was stamped on the item in order to set it and give it some longevity, such a mark would not be permanent. With the passing of time, marks applied over the glaze in this manner can become quite worn or rubbed off entirely. I inspected a bowl which appeared to be unmarked until held up to the light; then a very distinct outline of the mark could be seen. Because many 19th century porcelain manufacturers marked their wares before the vitreous (second) firing, those marks are sealed forever. For today's collectors, it would have been nice if RSP porcelains had been so marked.

It has been established that both Erdmann and Reinhold Schlegelmilch used the RSP mark at their respective Suhl and Tillowitz factories. I suggest that the time span for the RSP mark is from the late 1870s through the early 1900s with a more definite cut off date being 1914 or the beginning of World War I. (See Section 6, Plates 1 to 34 and Section 3 for Gaston Chronology of Schlegelmilch Marks.) My basis for the time span for the RSP mark is derived from several factors.

First of all, the founding dates of the factories (1861 for Erdmann's Suhl factory and 1869 for Reinhold's Tillowitz factory) encompassed a time period of unsettled circumstances in both Prussia and America. Wars were occurring in both areas during the latter part of this period (the American Civil War in this country). Thus, it is doubtful that very much exporting by the companies or importing by Americans was taking place until after 1870. Also the sheer mechanics of setting up a porcelain operation and getting it on a good production export basis takes time, sometimes several years. From trade advertisements of jewelry and department stores and catalog ordering companies, it is evident that the majority of RSP marked items came into this country during the late 1870s until circa 1914. It is noted that this time period also coincides with the peak of the German porcelain exporting industry. In 1906, 66% of the German porcelain production was exported with the industry employing approximately 40,000 workers.

Some people believe that the RSP mark was used only until 1871 when the Second German Empire was created. They suggest that at that time Germany rather than Prussia would have been used in the companies' back marks. Also some people say that the RSP mark was not used after 1891 because the McKinley Tariff Act of 1890 stated that the country of origin must be indicated on goods imported to this country. However, the McKinley Tariff Act did not require each *separate* piece of porcelain (or anything) to have a country of origin mark. Also it was common practice for European porcelain exporting companies to mark their wares with a country of origin name (in English) prior to 1890. Just because a mark has a country of origin as part of it does not arbitrarily mean that particualr item was made after 1891. Likewise, although the Act stated "country" of origin, that did not mean that "Germany" had to be substituted for "Prussia." Even if that had been the intent of the law, it had no bearing on the Prussia mark. Pieces which were made some years after 1890 still had the RSP mark. Examples which also have "Germany" stamped or incised in addition to the RSP mark, however, are probably in accordance with this Tariff Act. Notably the Peary Arctic Expedition commemorative pieces had to be made after 1909 (the date of the expedition). Thus it is evident that the RSP mark was not used only until 1871 (the time of the creation of the Second German Empire) or only until 1890 (the date of the McKinley Tariff Act).

Types of Objects

Items back stamped with the RSP mark can be broadly classified as art objects, dresser items, and table wares. Because of the decoration on dresser items and table wares, many of these items actually are considered to be art objects. These pieces were originally intended to be used for what they were. The prices were not so high as to prohibit persons with only moderate means from purchasing such wares. But it is doubtful that many collectors today really "use" their Prussia!

Bowls are the most commom example of RSP. Complete dinner services as well as cake, chocolate, tea, and coffee sets were also manufactured. Many table ware items which seem superflous to our life style today, were considered as basics. Mustard pots, syrup pitchers, and toothpick holders are a few examples. RSP items range in size from one inch pin boxes to 15 inch tankards and chargers, with a host of items in between. (Please refer to the alphabetical object index for a list of the various items pictured in this book.)

RSP Shapes

In order to make a piece of porcelain, the paste (raw ingredients) must be molded or shaped. Some porcelain is molded by hand, but most is poured into molds or forms, specifically designed to make the shape of a specific item. These forms can be used repeatedly, so a company can make numerous pieces which are the same. This process was a necessity for porcelain exporters during the 1900s, as it is today. Imagine the time and cost if each item of a dinner service, or even a tea set, had to be made entirely by hand. So, most examples of RSP were not one-of-a-kind objects. Few examples may be seen today of some molds, but this is due to other factors such as survival of the pieces primarily, or yet to be discovered items still packed away. The pieces may be *decorated* differently, but many of the shapes are the same. Sometimes the same shapes were duplicated in different sizes, or a particular mold design was repeated in another object. Often the decoration obscures the mold design, and it is not evident at first glance that one piece is exactly the same as another.

RSP molds are in fact one of the most fascinating aspects of this porcelain. If you imagine a piece in your mind without any decoration (blank so to speak) except for the decoration that was molded and shaped from the paste, the intricate designs and ornate shapes qualify such pieces as art porcelain. Although the same molds were used repeatedly, that does not take away from the fact that skilled artisans had to make the mold in the first place.

RSP molds are most often *rococo*, an ornately formed style fashioned with scroll work, flowers, or other shapes as part of the mold. Many RSP objects are quite thin while others are not so thin. The shape of the mold accounts partially for its thickness. To fashion ornate shapes, especially to "blow out" the sides of an object, the paste must be quite thin. If the paste is too thick, the object will look clumsy and heavy. The more simply shaped pieces are usually not so thin as the ornate examples. As the ornate molds are thinner, they are also apt to break more easily. The thinness really does not mean that one piece is better than another, although a high degree of translucency is desirable in fine porcelain.

The number of different RSP mold shapes seems to be endless. Because the molds are such an important part of this RSP story, however, I present a mold identification system for RSP pieces pictured in this book. No claim is made to have pictured and described all of the molds, although this is my ultimate goal. The Mold Identification System and how to use it, is in Section 6 which precedes the RSP photographs.

Decoration Methods

After the porcelain paste is molded, it is fired to a state of translucency. Objects can then be decorated before they are fired a second time (to a state of vitreosity). If the decoration is applied before the second firing, it is permanent or sealed and cannot be damaged (except through breakage, of course). This type of decoration is called *under glaze* decoration. If however, the decoration is applied after the second firing, so called *over glaze* decoration, the decor can be scratched or damaged, especially through time, although vitreous-type paints may have been used. Whether the decoration was applied over or under the glaze can be determined by feeling. If the design or pattern cannot be differentiated from the undecorated parts of an object, the decoration is under the glaze. The pieces will have a glass-like feel all over. If, however, the decoration has a texture, usually grainy, it has been decorated over the glaze. Check the undecorated portion of an object such as the bottom of a bowl or the inside of a vase, tankard or tea pot. These parts should have the glass-like feel, and when compared to the decorated parts, the difference in texture will be more obvious. (Note that the bases of some items such as trays and vases are unglazed, not vitreous, in order to give the objects more surface grippage.)

Porcelain is decorated, under or over the glaze, by one of three methods: handpainting, transfer designs or a combination of handpainting and transfer designs. Handpainting is the most costly method because of the time it takes, plus it requires a skilled artist. All porcelain was handpainted during the earliest years of the industry. Toward the latter part of the 1800s, however, most porcelain manufacturers were taking advantage of the transfer method. *Transfer* decorating is a process where a particualr design is made on paper, stone, or plates (lithography) and transferred to another object. The original design, like the mold, can be used over and over again on many types of objects. This process was developed first in England and was used on English earthenwares before it was used on porcelain. Transfer decoration is cheaper than handpainted designs. It also allows many objects to have identical decoration. Transfer decorating, just as using the same mold, is one of the main reasons for the rapid growth of the European porcelain exporting business. The process itself, though, is not really so simple as it may sound. Designs can be made, but they must be colored. The coloring process, if the decoration is to have more than one color, must go through several stages before the transfer is ready to use. Early transfer designs were hand colored; later ones were "printed."

Whether an object has been handpainted or decorated by transfer can be determined by examining it with a loupe or magnifying glass. If a uniform series of dots or lines can be seen, the piece has been decorated by transfer. If brush strokes or irregular lines are seen, the object was hand-painted. It was a common practice for porcelain manufacturers to combine these methods during the late 1800s, especially as gold frequently was used lavishly as part of the decoration. A main design was applied by transfer, but embellishments could be added by hand. Also *enamelling,* thickly applying paint in small areas creating a raised or relief appearance, was often used, particularly on floral designs.

Most RSP marked procelain was decorated by transfer design or a combination of transfer designs and hand applied gold or enamelling. The decoration was over the glaze. This accounts for the wear on some of the designs. Although some pieces were handpainted, very few were compared to those decorated by transfer. If pieces were handpainted at the factory, the word "Handpainted" is a part of the back mark (see Plate 6). Also some items marked "Handpainted" may actually refer only to enamelling or trim with the major design a transfer.

Not all porcelain was decorated at the factory, of course, and undecorated pieces are referred to as *blanks*. Many blanks manufactured by European porcelain companies were exported to this country during the late 1800s. These pieces were decorated by amateurs or professionals for their own use or to be sold. China painting was considered quite an accomplished art form at that time. Blanks with German, French, or Japanese marks which have been decorated by Americans from this era are quite common. RSP marked blanks, however, are quite rare, but they do exist. The examples I have personally seen had the RSP green mark with the mark of a decorating company. From some other double markings on RSP, it seems that perhaps some RSP blanks may also have been decorated by European or German decorators of the period. (See Section 4 for elaboration.)

Decoration Themes

The world of art encompasses many subjects and symbols. RSP porcelain was decorated with examples of popular subjects and artistic symbols. The decoration themes of RSP porcelain can be categorized as animal, bird, figural, floral, portrait, and scenic. In many instances pieces are decorated with more than one theme. That mixture of themes is only one of the many decorative characteristics that makes RSP so appealing to collectors.

Floral themes are the most common, while animal and fruit themes are the most scarce. Several of the portrait and figural themes were transfer decorations based on the original works of famous artists of the 18th and 19th centuries. At that time in history, the late 1800s, many porcelain manufacturers used such transfers on their products. The transfers are not precise replicas of the original paintings, although many of them have the artist's name or initials included in the picture as a signature. Such a signature implies that the artist actually painted that print and signed it. In the first place an exact print, made from the artist's original painting, would have the artist's signature if it appeared on the original painting. But the transfers were not made from the original paintings. The transfers were copied by other artists and print makers. They included the signature or the initials probably to indicate who had in fact been responsible for the original painting. One of the most common ideas or misstated interpretations concerning RSP decoration is that such pieces are artist signed. RSP porcelain which has a famous artist's name as part of the decoration was not decorated by that artist, nor the transfer made by that artist. Knowledge of the years when those particular artists lived would quickly show that idea to be incorrect. Most had died before RSP items were manufactured. The "signed" name, however, does cause confusion. Pieces are often advertised for sale, for example, which say, "such and such a plate, signed Lebrun." This makes it look as though Lebrun painted the plate and signed it. Experienced collectors, of course, are aware that this is not so. They know the pieces are not handpainted or that the transfers were not made by the artist. But new collectors may not be aware of this, and may be misled by advertisements which say "signed." The correct way to describe the piece is to say it is decorated "after the specific artist of the original painting." Many people also refer to the back marks as "signed" marks. A piece will be advertised which says, "signed R. S. Prussia." Technically the ad should say, "marked R. S. Prussia," but this misuse of the word "signed" is not as misleading, for the company that manufactured R. S. Prussia porcelain did in fact put the mark on the pieces, but it is a "stamped" mark, not drawn or written on each piece (even in the case of stamped signature marks) by the manufacturer himself!

The next section describes some of the more popular and common decoration subjects and symbols found on RSP. These are grouped under one of the six decoration themes. These subjects and other important terms used in the RSP photograph captions are discussed. Also consult the Index of Decoration Themes for color photograph examples of these themes and subjects.

Animal Themes

The rarest type of decoration on RSP, animals, includes items decorated with transfers of tigers, lions, gazelles, and giraffes. Most of these pieces quickly find their way to advanced collectors for they command the highest prices. Rumors suggest that these animal themes are being copied. This is not surprising due to the high prices such pieces can bring. If the authenticity of the piece is questionable (and I would say that all animal, especially jungle animal pieces should be questioned just as a rule of thumb), some clues or tips on ascertaining the authenticity can be suggested. First, inspect the back mark. Be sure that it is not a "fake" mark (see Collector's Problems, Section 4). If the mark is genuine, inspect the decoration carefully in a good light with a high powered magnifying glass. Determine if the animal decoration is handpainted. If it is handpainted, you can be certain that the piece was not decorated at the factory. The animal pieces should have transfer decorations. An authentic RSP mark cannot substantiate the piece either. A skilled artist would be able to add animal decoration to an old piece, especially one with little decoration or a piece with some part devoid of decoration such as the back of a vase, pitcher, or tankard. Because factory decorated pieces often employed several transfers or decorative themes, a piece with animal and other themes might not appear out of character at first.

If the animal decoration on a particular piece is a transfer, inspect the background coloring and finishes carefully. Are the colors subtle? Do they blend together and fit the theme? Feel of the animal design carefully to be sure it is not a new stick on type decal. Above all be wary of the price. If the article is too cheap, you can be sure it is not authentic. It is possible of course for someone to "find" a steal in an animal piece or any other piece if the owner is not aware of what the market value is. But any pieces sold at flea markets, gift type shops, antique shops or shows, or advertised as RSP animal pieces will not have an unknowledgeable seller. In the end, the responsibility for knowing what one has purchased rests with the buyer. All animal items should be inspected with the utmost scrutiny.

Other animal themes include a polar bear as part of the scene on some of the Admiral Peary commemorative items, and a stag with a surreal snowy background. The stag is based on a painting by an English artist, Sir Edwin Landseer (1802-1873) entitled "Monarch of the Glen." Sir Landseer's animal subjects were quite popular and copied by many print makers. He was a favorite of Queen Victoria and is known to have painted her portrait as well as portraits of her dogs! The Queen knighted Landseer in 1850.

Although barnyard animals should be placed ordinarly under the bird category, these particular birds—chickens, roosters, ducks, and turkeys—are commonly referred to as barnyard animals because several of these appear together in a group on various RSP items. A small house may be in the background, and sometimes the birds are facing a pheasant across a body of water. These birds also appear on pieces singly or in pairs.

Birds

In addition to the barnyard birds, this main category includes several species. The Swan is the most popular. Swans are featured singly, in pairs, or groups. They are often mixed with other transfers. Popular scenes are of swans on a lake with an "aisle of swans" on the back part of the lake which is narrow and flanked by evergreen trees. A gazebo or terrace scene also has swans as the central theme. Black swans appear on some RSP pieces, but such examples are quite rare. The swan, according to legends, is said to have loved music and to have sung a beautiful song when it died. Another legend says that the soul of a poet

entered the body of the swan. They are graceful and beautiful creatures at any rate which has made them a popular subject for artistic interpretation in many areas.

Flying Swallows, in small or large groups (some pieces show 13 in the air), are usually combined with barnyard animals or swan themes. The Snowbird is featured as part of a winter scene. The bird is perched on the icy bank of a pond with snow covered evergreens nearby. A house and mountains can be seen across the pond in the far background.

The Peacock and Peafowl are usually accompanied by trees or scenic backgrounds. Pheasants, parrots, birds of paradise, hummingbirds, blue birds, and the ostrich are other bird subjects found less frequently on RSP porcelain.

Figural Themes

Figural themes refer to decorations which portray whole figures rather than a bust, half figure, or cameo portrait. Many of the figural themes are based on some famous artist's work. Some information about the artist is included with some of these themes.

"The Melon Boys" and the "Dice Throwers" are perhaps the most popular figural themes on RSP porcelain. These scenes were based on paintings by Bartolomé Esteban Murillo, a Spanish artist (1618-1682). A series of beggar children paintings including "Boys Eating Melon," and "Boys Throwing Dice," are some of his most popular works. On RSP items, the "Melon Boys" shows two small boys in tattered clothing with one holding a piece of melon above his mouth with the other child looking at him. A dog and a basket of fruit are in the foreground. The "Dice Throwers" shows 3 boys: two are kneeling at a game of dice on a stone, while a third child is standing, eating a piece of fruit with a dog beside him. The die was a symbol of the Passion for the soldiers who cast lots for Christ's tunic. In Greek mythology, the children of Venus are those who played games of chance.

The pieces of RSP which are decorated with these themes do not always have all of the scene on each piece. Sometimes only one of the melon boys is shown, or sometimes the third child in the "Dice Throwers" appears alone on pieces.

"The Cage" is a romantic theme featuring a boy and a girl sitting in a wooded area with flowers and a bird cage in the foreground. This scene is from the painting, "The Cage" by François Boucher (1703-1770), court painter to King Louis XV. He was noted for such romantic subjects as well as landscapes, portraits, and mythological themes. His series of the four seasons, "The Charms of Spring, Summer, Autumn, Winter," are not the same women pictured as the Four Seasons on RSP porcelain (see the portrait Themes section below). His works were quite popular during the century following his death. His works served as the basis for many copyists.

"Diana the Huntress" and "Flora" are two mythological figural themes on RSP items. These subjects were based on the paintings by the French portrait painter, Nattier (1685-1766). Nattier was also a painter at the court of Louis XV. "Madame Adelaide as Diana," and "Madame Henriette as Flora," are two of his popular works.

Diana, according to mythology, was one of the goddesses of Olympus. Her portrayal as The Huntress was only one of the several legends connected with her. As the Huntress, she was often shown with a bow, a quiver of arrows, hounds, or deer. She was also sometimes pictured resting after the hunt; this is the particular type of scene on RSP objects.

Flora was the Italian goddess of flowers and symbol of spring. She is usually portrayed as a woman with flowers. RSP pieces show a lady reclining, holding a floral garland. Multi-colored flowers are in the foreground.

"Peace Bringing Plenty," is based on the painting "La Paix Qui Ramené L'Abondance," by Madame Lebrun (see the Portrait Themes in this section). The symbol of Peace is usually portrayed by a dove and less frequently by a woman, as in Lebrun's painting. Peace is a fair-haired maiden bringing a basket of fruit to a dark-haired maiden.

"The Peary Arctic Expedition" (1909) is featured on RSP objects to commemorate that historic event. One scene features warmly clad figures with an igloo and the American Flag. Another shows a figure on skis with huskies confronting a polar bear with a snow and ice background.

"Victorian Vignettes" refer to several figural themes, often in pastoral settings with figures in Victorian dress. A boy and a girl at a well; a boy and a girl with sheep; a boy serenading or reading to a girl; and a lady watering flowers are a few examples.

Floral Themes

The most common decorations on RSP porcelain are floral. Even if the central theme is a portrait or a figural subject, floral designs are also often a part of the total decoration. Roses in all colors seem to have been the favorite flower, but other flowers such as poppies, snowballs, dogwood, iris, and several forms of lilies were also popular. Sometimes the particular flower cannot be identified as one which exists in nature. Transfer makers and mold modelers often used their own imagination to shape or outline a flower. Dogwood blossoms appear in a realistic design as one pattern on pieces and in a surreal design on other pieces. (See Plates 175 and 213 for examples.)

Another floral characteristic of a surreal nature is seen on numerous examples of RSP. This is in the form of background design where floral or leaf images look like reverse shadows; that is, a darker color outlines a floral or leaf shape. The shape remains uncolored or else is a much lighter version of the same shade (see Plate 44). Or the floral or leaf designs may be in different colors, but they are designed in a hazy fashion, not clearly and definitely outlined, rather "ghostly" type images. These floral designs may not be easily recognized on a piece—in fact such designs are really unobtrusive—but this type of floral imagery is one of the most distinctive decorative traits of RSP porcelain.

The following terms and theme name are used in the picture descriptions of RSP floral items:

Bkgrd—background;
Dogwood—realistic blossoms;
Floral—floral decoration, often a combination of different types of flowers;
Foliage—leaves or greenery;
Hanging Basket—small basket filled with multi-colored roses with a ribbon handle and rose on top; the basket seems suspended in air;

Laurel Chain—floral pattern with green leaves and yellow centers in chain form;
Mixed—more than one type of flower;
Multi-colored—more than one color of flower;
Reflecting Poppies and Daisies—pink poppies and white daisies reflected in a pond;
Reflecting Water Lilies—water lilies reflected in a pond;
Shaded—color changes, from dark to light or vice versa;
Shadow Flowers—surreal floral images;
Sitting Basket—a large cane basket with handle filled with multi-colored roses;
Surreal—unreal, dreamy, floral designs;
Surreal Dogwood—large white floral shapes without a true dogwood form, usually having gold enameled centers.

Fruit Themes

Almost as scarce as animal themes, fruit decorations on RSP items are quite desirable. It is not readily apparent why the fruit themes are so seldom seen. Most of the fruit decoration is on bowls, tankards, and trays. Perhaps the decoration did not seem as fitting for many items as some of the other themes. Also it is obvious that fruit bowls had this type of decoration, and this type of bowl is likely to have had as much use as any other piece. As a result, many would have been broken as a matter of course.

The fruit themes are composed of a variety of fruits. Grapes of some type are part of most transfers. Pears, apples, and oranges are usually combined with the grapes. I have not seen just one type of fruit on any piece.

Portrait Themes

Certainly, portrait themes are one of the favorites of RSP collectors. The portraits are primarily of women. Some of the subjects are of famous people, based on paintings by specific artists. Other portraits are representations only of people typical of a historical era.

For generations, "The Four Seasons" were a popular decoration. These seasons, denoting the seasonal changes of the year, have been portrayed by artists throughout history. Certain symbols were used to identify each of the four seasons. Spring was often symbolized by a young woman holding flowers or having flowers in her hair. Spring might also be represented by a young man and young woman with flowers or birds in the scene. Summer was often portrayed by a woman holding corn or fruit, or by reapers in the field. Grapes and vine leaves were associated with Autumn. Winter reflected protection against the cold. This season was sometimes presented as an old man by the fire, or people ice skating. Snow of course, was usually a part of the picture.

It is not surprising that the Four Seasons pictured on RSP exemplify some of the same characteristics as other contemporary renditions of the theme. Beautiful women, elegantly but scantily gowned, are shown, each with specific symbols to represent her season. Spring has flowers in her hair and a flowering dogwood branch in her arms. Winter's arms are clasped in front of her as a shield from the cold; surreal snow covered trees (note this type of tree is seen on other RSP items also), snowflakes, and a holly branch complete the scene. Summer holds red poppies near her head, and a wheat field serves as the background. Autumn has a yellow-peach rose at the top of her gown; the wind appears to be blowing her hair and scarf as well as the leaves swirling around her.

On RSP items, one season is usually the central theme, but sometimes all four seasons appear together, in cameo or medallion form, with one season or some other theme as the central subject. The Four Seasons may have different backgrounds and different finishes on various types of objects. Bowls, plates, and trays appear to have been manufactured as specific sets of the seasons. Collectors are anxious to acquire a matching set. Chocolate, tea, and coffee services seem to have been decorated with the same season on each piece, however. The Seasons are often seen on some of the most elaborate RSP molds.

"Madame Lebrun" is one of the most frequent portrait subjects that was used on RSP. She was not only a beautiful woman, but also a famous French artist. The decoration transfers of her portrait on RSP, in fact, are based on her self portraits. Madame Lebrun's (1755-1842) full name was Marie Louise Elisabeth Vigeé. Her maiden name, Vigeé, is usually included in identifying her works. Madame Lebrun was a favorite artist of Queen Marie Antoinette. She painted many portraits of the Queen as well as portraits of other beautiful women of the era. In addition to the self portraits, another transfer on RSP which is based on her original painting is "Peace Bringing Plenty" (see Figural themes).

One of two self portraits of Madame Lebrun are found on many different types of RSP items. In one, she is wearing a white cap with a white ruff around her neck. Sometimes versions of this portrait show part of her gown as well. In the second, she does not have on her cap, but she has a white ribbon in her hair. The white neck of her gown can usually be seen. These transfers appear alone on items, or they are combined with other portrait cameos or medallions.

Another famous painting by the artist is "Madame Vigeé-Lebrun et sa fille" (Madame Lebrun and her Daughter). This painting portrays the artist holding a young girl in her arms. This particular subject has been seen on porcelain pieces which were either unmarked or had the mark of another factory. From the mold of the unmarked version, it is difficult to attribute definitely such a piece as an RSP product.

"Madame Récamier" (1777-1849) is another French beauty pictured on RSP. Her full name was Jeanne Françoise Julie Adelaide Bernard. In 1793, she married a wealthy banker much older than she. After his eventual financial ruin, a marriage was arranged for her with Prince August of Prussia, but this never occurred. She was noted for her "salons," where she entertained important social and political figures of the time. The decoration transfer of her portrait on RSP was styled after the painting by Baron François Pascal Simon Gérard (1710-1837). He was born in Rome, but he is known as a French portrait painter. He painted for Napoleon, and he was court painter to the Bourbons after the Restoration. His painting of Madame Récamier in 1802 helped spread his fame. He was made a baron by King Louis XVIII in 1819.

Other portrait subjects found on RSP items include the Polish Countess and writer, "Anna Potocka," and an Italian Countess, "Catherine Litta." Countess Potocka is portrayed with long red-brown curls and ribbon. Countess Litta is looking over her shoulder, an unusual and striking pose. "Napoleon," "Josephine," and "Queen Louise" are subjects less frequently seen on RSP objects.

Scenic Themes

Secnic themes are outside scenes. Small figural images are usually a part of these scenes. The varous scenic types of decoration are found on all types of RSP porcelain.

The "Castle" or "Church" scene also could be called the "Village" scene. It is difficult to determine actually if the dominant building in the picture is a church or a castle. Either would have been considered appropriate subjects for the time. This building has a tall spire shaped roof with a cross on top. There are several other buildings close to it. A man can be seen walking on a path toward the buildings. A body of water is to his right. As collectors use the term "Castle" more frequently to describe this scene than "Church," that is the term used in my picture captions.

The "Mill" refers to a particualr decoration of a water mill and an adjoining cottage by a stream. The figure of a woman wearing an apron and a kerchief on her head complete the scene. The water mill was a popular artist theme especially during the 1800s. A famous picture printer of the era was George Baxter (1804-1864). His print, entitled, "The Old Watermill," was based on a poem by Eliza Cook. The miller's house, the mill, and the miller's boy were the subjects of the poem. The transfer on RSP is not the same as Baxter's print, but the mill and adjoining cottage are quite similar.

Pieces with the mill scene are often companion pieces to those with castle scenes. Evidently, sets of items were made with all pieces decorated with the same theme—either the castle or the mill. These may have been purchased as mixed sets, however, for it is common to see matching pieces of a teaset (all with the same mold, for example) with some pieces decorated with the castle scene and others with the mill scene. Of course, it is also possible that the matching pieces were lost or broken and, over the years, the broken sets have been joined up with pieces having the other decoration. Because the molds and colors match, they form a "set" in either way.

The "Cottage" is in the same category as the Mill and Castle scenes. A quaint house with a thatched roof is the focal point. A small boy with a pack on his back can be seen going out of the front door. Perhaps this is a representation of the miller's boy and house also.

The "Sheepherder (#1)" refers to the particular scene portraying a figure with sheep in the foreground. Pink flowering trees dominate the scene. A house and mountains are in the far background.

The "Sheepherder (#2)" or "Shepherd" shows a larger figure of a man with a staff and flock of sheep. Tall white birch trees are a distinguishing characteristic of this picture. A house is also part of the scene, but it is not the same as in Sheepherder #1. (Note that another Sheepherder decoration is found on R.S. Germany marked pieces, see Plate 537).

The "Man in the Mountain" presents a striking mountain and water decoration. The side view of the mountain in the foreground seems to resemble the profile of a man's face. A sailboat on the lake completes the scene.

Other scenic themes include large ships with masted sails. These are often referred to as "Schooners." At least two different versions of these ships are found on RSP items.

The "Evergreens" are included as a form of scenic decoration. These are the tall cedar trees which are found alone on RSP items or combined with other decorative subjects, such as swans or barnyard animals.

Background Colors

Another distinguishing characteristic of RSP is the background colors. These colors are not the "finish" on an object, but are part of the decorative themes. The usual subject of decoration was not left unadorned. A portrait or scenic transfer, for example, was not simply placed on the white vitreous glaze of the object and considered finished. Background colors were necessary to highlight the central theme. These colors were applied over the glaze by transfer methods just like the decoration transfers. The background colors are not to be confused with glazes which are a type of finish. Both, background colors and glazes, of course, can be used to decorate an object. The surreal floral and leaf images are a part of the background colors.

Interesting features of the background colors are the many different shades of a particular color or combination of colors which were used. Primarily in brown, blue, green, or yellow, these background colors varied from very dark to very light shades. Other colors such as red, pink, lavender, and orange were treated in the same way although these are not so prevalent. The colors often have a mottled appearance on some pieces. Colors were also combined: the backgrounds are not all necessarily shades of just one color. Some specific subjects are associated with certain background colors. The Mill and Castle scenes, for example, are usually in brown or blue-green tones. This unique characteristic of background colors really defies proper word description. It is best understood and appreciated by viewing the photographs.

Finishes

One of the most important characteristics of RSP products is the finish decoration. Finish is defined as a particular *surface* quality of an object. After a piece of porcelain is decorated (or sometimes before) with a specific subject and background, another type of glaze (a vitreous or glassy coating) can be applied. There are many different types and colors of glazes which result from specific materials used to achieve the desired effect. The glazes can be applied over all of the surface of an object or just on certain parts. For example, a portrait item might have an irridescent glaze surrounding it, but the portrait itself would not have this glaze. Sometimes only the border

or small parts of the border have a different or additional finish from the rest of the body of the piece. Some of the glazes or finishes on RSP porcelain include the following:

Glossy—a shiny finish with a slick look (either high gloss, very shiny or lacquered in appearance, or semi-gloss with only a light sheen);

Irridescent—glazes which have different colors that appear to change with varying amounts of light;

Lustre—a metallic glaze which has a shiny, irridescent effect;

Matte—a dull finish, not lustrous or shiny;

Pearl—a shiny finish, usually white, and not iridescent;

Pearl Button—a hard pearl finish which resembles a pearl button;

Pearlized—an iridescent, lustre type finish;

Satin—a semi-matte glaze, usually white, resembling satin in look and texture;

Solid Colors—metallic glazes composed of only one color such as red, green, or cobalt blue;

Tiffany—a brown, green, or bronze iridescent glaze which resembles Tiffany art glass;

Watered Silk—a smudged color effect, usually on satin finishes, which resembles a water spot on silk or satin.

In addition to the different types of glazes used on RSP, gold was an important finishing touch on many pieces. Objects were gilded on the borders (lightly or heavily), on bases, handles, and feet, or on outlines of designs formed in the mold. A brief look at the photographs immediately shows how much gold was actually a part of the decor of so many items. One specific type of gold decoration is referred to as the *Tapestry* finish. Parts of an object, borders or medallions, rarely the entire surface, have small bead forms painted gold all over the circumscribed area. *Stippling* is the term used to describe this form of beading. Stippled designs were occasionally painted or glazed with colors other than gold.

Objects may also have gold *stencilled* designs: repetitive patterns made in stencil form and painted gold. These designs are usually applied as outer or inner border enhancement. Another use of gold was in spray or mottled form over the surface or on certain parts of the surface. Gold was an important part of the decorating process for most 19th century porcelain manufacturers. This is understandabe for gold imparts such as a rich look. Porcelain produced during the later part of the first quarter of the 20th century, however, was not lavishly decorated with gold. Silver trims on porcelain came into style during this latter period. Silver trim was of course less expensive but usually less attractive than gold finishes.

RSP porcelain objects present such a beautiful overall effect, that it is perhaps easy to look at a piece without really *seeing* it. If you take the time to examine a piece thoroughly, from the intricate mold designs and translucency to the decorative subjects, colorful backgrounds, unique finishes, and gold embellishments, you will have an even greater appreciation for this beautiful porcelain.

3.
Other Suhl and Tillowitz Factory Marks

Suhl and E.S. Marks (see Plates 16, 17, 19 to 23)

In addition to the RSP mark, Erdmann's factory at Suhl, established in 1861, is associated with marks which have the initials E.S. or the words Suhl or Thuringia. Some of the E.S. marks also use the word "Saxe." Other marks incorporate the year "1861" as part of the mark. Because of the historical nature of the area of the factory's location, such marks suggest that they were the first marks used by the Schlegelmilch Suhl factory. The town of Suhl was located in a region known as Thuringia in the Germanic area of Europe. Thuringia, however, was identified as part of the Germanic state of Saxony from the late 1400s until the end of World War I. Part of the Thuringian region, however, was conquered by the Prussians in 1815. From that time, those conquered provinces were known as Prussian provinces in Saxony. Thus, there is a basis for all four words (Suhl, Thuringia, Saxe, Prussia) appearing independently in the company's marks. The chronology of these marks cannot be established, however, on the basis of the historical nature of the area. The examples of items with a Saxe or Suhl mark in fact appear to be later than those with a Prussia mark.

The style and decoration of pieces with these marks are basically different in shape and decor than the RSP marked pieces. The art form changed from the rococo (the basic RSP style) to the art nouveau circa 1895. The art nouveau era was a short period, losing its peak after about fifteen years. The style emphasized an elegant flowing line rather than the convoluted rococo shapes. More individual effort in decorating, basically handpainting, was also a prevalent characteristic of pieces typified by this style. Many pieces marked "Prov Saxe," do, in fact, exemplify this style in mold form, and also many with that mark have handpainted decoration. Although the Prov Saxe mark also has the word Germany as part of it, as do several other E.S. Marks, that does not mean that the mark was used only after the end of World War I when Prussia was no longer an independent state. Rather, it is clear that Reinhold was using R.S. Germany as his mark prior to the beginning of the war as noted in pre-World War I advertisements. The word "Germany" could logically have been used in any mark after 1871 when the second German Empire was formed with Prussia as a member state.

After the peak of the art nouveau style, circa 1905, styles returned to more classical and simple forms. Various pieces with Suhl or E.S. markings show evidence of this trend. Many Suhl marked pieces are decorated with a classical or mythological theme, often with transfers based on the style of Angelica Kauffmann (1741-1807). She was a famous artist of that earlier period noted for such scenes. Some Suhl marked pieces have her name or initials appearing as part of the transfer. Of course, I discussed previously in Section 2 how such artists did not personally decorate the pieces or even prepare the transfers.

Another subject of decoration found on pieces with Prov Saxe or Suhl marks is a "Gibson" girl. This subject was based on the series of drawings by an American artist, Charles Dana Gibson (1867-1944), entitled, "The Widow and Her Friends." These drawings date from the 1890s. The works were very popular, and the Royal Doulton Company in England made lithographs of the drawings to be used on plates manufactured by that company in the early 1900s. The Schlegelmilch marked pieces with "Gibson" girl subjects were not the same as those used by Doulton, and in all likelihood were made at a later date than the Doulton lithographs. However, this particular subject of decoration helps to substantiate that these marks (Prov Saxe and Suhl) were not the first marks of the Suhl company or earlier than the RSP mark. In general, it appears that the Suhl and E.S. marks that are commonly seen on porcelain items in this country date from the early 1900s until the dissolution of the Suhl factory in the 1920s.

World conditions of course influenced the Suhl factory. During the war years, there would have been little, if any, porcelain exporting. After the war, the firm would have required considerable time to get production operating on an export scale once more. There was not as large a demand for art objects or fancy table china following World War I. Simple styles and utilitarian wares in the form of basic table china were in demand. Following the end of World War I in 1918 to the company's closing during the 1920s, it is apparent that a much smaller amount of the company's products would have reached this country. Hence, fewer examples with the Suhl or Prov Saxe marks are found today.

Regarding the use of the year "1861" in Erdmann's marks, it is evident that this year denoted only the date of origin of the factory. It does not mean that pieces with such a mark were made in that year. A period of time must elapse during which a company becomes established with a wide market for its products before a mark is implemented to incorporate the date of the founding of the company. When a factory is established for manufacturing porcelain, some time passes, even years, before production is running smoothly. There are many processes connected with the production, ranging from acquiring the raw materials to the molding, firing, decorating, packaging, marketing, and distributing, before a piece of clay becomes a beautiful porcelain object with a home in a foreign country! The marks with this date are (1) composed of a cartouch with the name Schlegelmilch, 1861, Suhl, inside and a crown above, (2) Erdmann Schlegelmilch in script above 1861 with Prussia in script below, and (3) a crown with 1861 above, the initials E.S. and Germany printed below the crown (see Plate 23). With the exception of this latter mark, the first two plus a mark with Suhl inside a half-wreath at the top and a double-lined semi-circle at the bottom to form a logo, are to my knowledge marks that are only seen in reference sources. Lack of available pieces with these marks, thus, makes it difficult to know when such marks might have been used. They, in fact, might have been early marks, or marks used only on wares which were not exported. (If readers could provide photographs of both such objects and their marks, they would be appreciated.)

Bird and Eagle Marks (see Plate 18)

Several marks associated with Erdmann's Suhl factory have a bird or eagle as the main part of the mark. With the exception of Mark 18 (Plate 18), such marks also seem to be only in books of marks, and like the Suhl marks mentioned above, are rarely seen on objects available today. The example shown in Plate 18 is the only mark of this type that was available for photographing. The other "bird" marks include (1) an oval shape with the figure of a bird in flight and the initials E.S. in script, (2) an oval shape with a similar bird, the initials E.S. and Suhl printed underneath the figure and a ribbon tied in a bow above the mark, and (3) a circle with the printed words "Suhla" above, Germany below, and the initials E.S. The figure of a bird is inside the circle. Again, it is conceivable that such marks were used prior to the RSP mark or used only on wares not exported to this country. Absence of either the word Prussia or Germany in the first two marks also adds to the confusion about when such marks were used, as does the lack of available pieces with those marks. Because pieces for photographing with those marks were not found, those marks are not included in this edition. (Photographs of such examples would be welcomed.)

Other Tillowitz Factory Marks

In addition to the RSP mark, Reinhold's porcelain factory in Tillowitz, Upper Silesia, used several other marks through the years. Some brief historical facts should be discussed in order to gain a clearer understanding of Reinhold's company. Most sources agree with the date of 1869 as the founding year of his company. Some sources, however, place the date as 1896. I think that this might in fact be a printing error. It is easy to transpose the 6 and 9. The Tillowitz location in Upper Silesia was quite a distance from the Suhl factory in Thuringia. It appears that Reinhold settled in Tillowitz to take advantage of the natural resources available there for producing porcelain. The area of Upper Silesia had historically been a Polish land, but circa 1742, the region came under the domination of Prussia. The German people were encouraged to settle and start businesses in Upper Silesia because of the wealth of natural resources located there, not only for porcelain, but coal, iron, and other minerals as well.

Reinhold's factory was established to take advantage of the foreign export market rather than to serve the local or home market. He is noted to have exported his wares not only to America and Canada, but to England and France also. The porcelain he manufactured was considered of excellent quality. He produced what the Europeans refer to as "luxury" porcelain (art objects) and fine table wares. Products with his marks appear to have been exported to this country chiefly from the mid 1870s until the mid 1930s with little if any exported during the years of the Second World War. Following the end of World War II, the location of the company became a part of Poland rather than Germany. Although 1956 is shown by one source as the end of the R.S. wreath mark, few examples of the company's products appear to have been exported to this country from 1945 until that date. More discussion of these later dates is presented in this section under the R.S. Poland Mark.

During this considerable time span of the company's existence, several marks were used. Some of these do appear in some respects to reflect the historical events of the era. Other marks, however, are more ambiguous. Each mark is discussed below.

Steeple Marks (see Plates 1, 2 and 3)

Based on obvious facts, it appears that Reinhold was the entrepreneur of the Schlegelmilch family porcelain business. Namely, he established a new factory away from his brother's location, he exported to foreign countries, he set up marketing offices in the United States, and his name rather than Erdmann's is associated with American trade advertisements for the company's products. Thus it seems reasonable to suggest that marks of the Tillowitz company may have been the first to appear on exported goods rather than marks of the Suhl factory, and in fact precede the RSP wreath mark. The R.S. Steeple marks have certain characteristics which make them appear as the earliest marks on exported items.

The Steeple marks are formed simply, and they are in solid colors: red or green. "Germany" or "Prussia" appears below the mark. Pieces so marked are usually ornately fashioned and richly decorated. Many of the pieces are decorated with cobalt blue, a color popular during the 1870s for decorating porcelain. It is difficult to say which of the steeple marks (Prussia or Germany) was first used. Logically, it would seem that the Prussia steeple mark would have been first. It does not seem reasonable to suggest, however, that the Germany steeple mark would have been used after the RSP wreath and star mark. In all likelihood probably both steeple marks were used prior to the RSP mark or simultaneously with it. One mold (see Plate 478) is noted to have been found with either one of three marks: R.S. Steeple Germany; R.S. Steeple Prussia; or R.S. Prussia wreath and star red mark. This evidently indicates a transition period for the marks.

Because relatively few pieces with Steeple marks surface today, it seems that the Steeple marks were not used for any long period of time. I suggest circa mid 1870s to circa 1880 for the Steeple marks, followed by the RSP mark of both the Suhl and Tillowitz factories. As noted in Section 2, the RSP mark should fall in the time period of the late 1870s through the early 1900s, prior to World War I. (Note that in the photographs of R.S. Steeple marked items, some unmarked pieces are attributed to these marks because of their shape and decoration rather than to the RSP mark.)

R.S. Germany Marks (see Plates 24 to 29)

The most common mark associated with Reinhold's factory is a mark similar to the RSP wreath and star mark. The mark differs, however, because "Germany" instead of "Prussia" appears below the mark, and the mark is always a solid color. The mark is usually under glaze as opposed to the over glaze RSP mark. The R.S. Germany (RSG) mark rather than the RSP mark is the mark that all but one of my foreign references show for this company. The other sources show the RSP mark only for Erdmann's Suhl factory. From the double markings of RSP and RSG (see Plates 7, 8, and 9), it is evident that Reinhold did use the RSP mark. It is not clear, however, which factory first used the RSP mark.

The forms and decoration of porcelain products marked R.S. Germany generally show a decided change from objects marked RSP. Like the Suhl factory, the Tillowitz factory was influenced by world conditions and prevailing art trends. The change in style is evident when the Steeple marked rococo pieces and the Germany marked RSP type pieces are compared to the majority of items with RSG marks which are molded simply and decorated more subtley. The RSG pieces found in the same or similar types of ornate molds as RSP pieces, and those with RSP decorations such as the Mill scene or Lebrun self-portraits seem to indicate a transition period for both the marks and the type of form and decoration. Many RSG pieces also reflect the art deco or art moderne trend of the 1920s. The market for porcelain during the early 1900s was geared highly to lovely table china more than to art pieces. The Tillowitz company seems to have concentrated on this type of production from the early 1900s.

Many RSG pieces in the form of table items, however, can be considered art objects because of their decoration and style. Many are handpainted and have a factory "Handpainted" mark in addition to the RSG mark. As noted in Section 2, however, the "Handpainted" mark sometimes refers only to hand applied trim or enamelling. Floral handpainted subjects are desirable as are certain RSG themes such as the "Sheepherder," "Man with Horses," and "Cottage" scene. The high gloss finish and art deco shape of many of these pieces make such examples highly collectable.

Many more RSG pieces than RSP items were handpainted. Sometimes there is no artist signature on factory handpainted items. If the piece has an artist's signature, but does not have an RSG mark with "Handpainted" as part of it, the piece was a blank decorated by someone else, probably in America. RSP blanks are quite rare, but many RSG blanks are on the market. These blanks with the RSG mark are handpainted or occasionally still "blank" or undecorated. The mark of a decorating company may appear as a double mark with the RSG factory mark. The Pickard mark is the one most commonly associated with RSG blanks. This company was a decorating studio for porcelain. It was established in 1894 in Illinois and is still in operation. The studio decorated the blanks of many European porcelain companies. Often such pieces have an artist's signature in addition to the Pickard and RSG mark. Pieces with the Pickard and RSG mark can be dated (within a small time span) by the Pickard mark on the item because a definite chronology is available for Pickard marks. Other professional decorating companies and artists added their own signature or mark to RSG pieces. Normally if a piece is signed on the front, the work was that of a professional (proud of his work); if the piece is signed on the back, the painter was probably an amateur!

Other markings that may accompany RSG marks are those of department stores. It was common during the early 1900s for American companies such as department or jewelry stores to order porcelain from European factories and have their name added to the factory mark. Particular pattern or design marks may also appear as double marks with the factory mark. The "Cottonplant" decoration is an example of this latter type of mark with the work "Cottonplant" double marked with the RSG mark.

R.S. Tillowitz Marks (see Plates 24 and 30)

There are several known Tillowitz marks for Reinhold's Tillowitz factory. One is a fancy script mark with the initials "R." and "S." on either side of a fancy "T" followed by the rest of the letters of the word with the end of the "z" circling back to the beginning of the word. This mark is noted as a painted rather than a printed mark. Lack of examples with this mark make it impossible to assess the time period when it was used. It is probable that it, like the other marks which are rarely if ever seen on examples on the market, was either an early mark or one used infrequently on exported wares.

Another mark containing the word "Tillowitz" is Reinhold's script mark which accompanies the RSP mark. This is the most commonly seen Tillowitz mark. The RSG wreath mark may also have Tillowitz as well as Silesia or Germany or both under it in many instances. Another mark is like the RSG wreath mark except only the word Tillowitz appears under the mark. Many pieces with the R.S. Tillowitz wreath mark show the influence of the art deco style. Some of these pieces are quite outstanding, especially the factory handpainted items. Such pieces with the RS Tillowitz wreath mark appear to date after 1918 or the end of World War I.

R.S. Silesia Mark (see Plates 31 and 32)

This mark also is similar to the RSG wreath mark except Silesia rather than Germany appears under the mark or Royal may appear above the mark. This mark also seems to date after 1918. Such marks with only Silesia or Tillowitz are understandable in light of the unsettled boundary conditions of the region following World War I. (See R.S. Poland in this section for elaboration.) The R.S. Silesia marked pieces are sometimes not decorated very well, and some are evidently blanks with the quality of decoration varying according to the artistic capabilities of the artist. Most of the pieces with this mark are in the form of table wares.

R.S. Poland Mark (see Plates 33 and 34)

Reinhold Schlegelmilch's factory is credited with the R.S. wreath "Made in (German) Poland" mark also. Many collectors date this mark from 1916 to 1918, because that time coincides with the time period when Germany occupied *part* of Poland during World War I. Extensive research, however, does not substantiate that date for the R.S. Poland mark. Historical evidence places the mark at a much later time, circa the end of World War II. A brief history of the area of location of the factory and world events prior to World War I until the end of World War II are discussed below in order to show the basis for my disagreement with the 1916 to 1918 period for the mark.

Prior to World War I, Poland was divided between Russia, Austria, and Germany. In 1915, Germany invaded and occupied the Russian part of Poland. Tillowitz, the location of Reinhold's factory, was not a part of that occupied territory. Tillowitz is in Upper Silesia. Upper Silesia historically had been part of Poland (until circa the mid 1300s), and the people of the area were predominantly Polish centuries later, even though they had been ruled by other countries after the mid 1300s. The Prussians captured Upper Silesia from Austria (the Hapsburgs) in 1742. From that time, the area was considered Prussian (or German) territory. When Germany occupied the Russian part of Poland in 1915, that did not change the status of Upper Silesia. There would have been no reason for the porcelain company to change its mark from Germany to Poland.

At the end of the war, in 1918, Poland was declared a nation in her own right. Lands formerly held by the Germans were to be returned to Poland. As Upper Silesia had historically been Polish and was predominantly populated with Polish people, it appeared at first that the whole Upper Silesian area would be returned to Poland. Germany, however, would not agree to this. Many German businesses and industries including, of course, many German people had settled in this region. Thus, it was agreed and stipulated by the Treaty of Versailles that the question of Upper Silesia would be decided by plebescite or popular vote.

According to President Woodrow Wilson, it would be a question of self-determination—let the people decide whether they wanted to be a part of Germany or a part of Poland. These elections, however, were not held until 1921. When the elections were held, Germany received about 75% of the Upper Silesian area which contained about 57% of the population. Poland received the smaller portion of

land, but that land contained the major portion of the area's resources: coal mines, iron ore deposits, zinc and steel factories, for example. Germany and Poland signed a fifteen year free trade agreement concerning the German and Polish parts of Upper Silesia after the boundaries were determined. Tillowitz remained on the German side, thus continuing to be a part of Germany.

Germany, under Hitler, though, in 1939, occupied Polish Silesia. Thus for a short time, Germany again controlled all of Upper Silesia. At the end of World War II in 1945, however, all territories east of the Oder-Neisse (rivers) line came under the administration of Poland. All of this territory was eventually annexed by Poland. This area did include the former German Silesian provinces. As a result, Tillowitz was under Polish administration, and eventually became a part of Poland rather than Germany. Hence the use of a mark like the R.S. Made in (German) Poland mark would be the proper mark for that time for an area which was formerly German but under the control of Poland.

Furthermore, in addition to these world history facts, a Polish reference source (Chróscicki, 1974), indicates that Reinhold's company used the German name "Tillowitz" and the R.S. wreath and star mark to mark his wares from circa 1869 to 1956. He notes that circa 1945 the town of Tillowitz came under the administration of Poland. He shows that after 1956, the company was using a mark similar to the R.S. wreath mark. This mark has the wreath and star, but the initials P.T. instead of R.S. The initials stand for Poland, Tulowice (the Polish spelling of Tillowitz). The words "Tulowice, Made in Poland," are under the mark. The similarities between this mark and the R.S. wreath "Made in (German) Poland" mark are quite obvious.

With this particular mark (Wreath with the initials P.T., Tulowice, Made in Poland) attributed as dating from 1956 by a Polish reference plus the history of the area, makes it highly unlikely that the R.S. "Made in (German) Poland" mark that we see infrequently was used from 1916 to 1918. The time period between 1945 and 1956 is a more logical one. Marks 33 and 34 (Plates 33 and 34) seem to represent the transition period for the RSG and R.S. Poland marks with the R.S. Poland mark being added to wares already marked RSG or Germany. No date is given for the close of the Tillowitz factory. It appears that the factory came under the control of the socialist government of Poland in 1956.

Regardless of the date of manufacture, R.S. Poland marked pieces are quite rare. This would stand to reason because following World War II little export business was conducted. The pieces with the R.S. Poland mark are usually of good quality and handsomely decorated. The styles and decoration of the items so marked are predominantly classical or simple rather than ornate or rococo. Most pieces with this mark are in the form of art objects such as vases and jardinieres, rather than tableware items. The molds do not help to date the pieces because they are primarily simple. Some of the molds are the same or similar to RSG molds which were used from the early 1900s through the 1930s. Such simple molds could, of course, have been made during any time period. See Section 7 for my suggested chronology of Schlegelmilch Suhl and Tillowitz Factory Marks.

4.
Collector's Problems

THE PROBLEMS CONFRONTING collectors of Schlegelmilch porcelain are really confined to the RSP red mark, rather than to any other R.S. or E.S. mark. Consulting the price guide, it will be evident even to the noncollector, that the porcelain objects with these other marks do not yet command near the prices that the RSP marked items do. Thus it is not lucrative or advantageous to reproduce these other marks or copy the type and decor of porcelains with these other marks. Another detriment to the reproducing of pieces with other R.S. or E.S. marks is that many examples are not that distinguishable from other European porcelains manufactured by other companies during the same time period. As a result such unmarked pieces cannot be definitely attributed to one of these other marks. The molds are not that distinctive as opposed to the RSP molds. The decoration and finishes on some unmarked pieces resemble RSG items; but without the mark, it is indeed possible that the piece was manufactured by another company. Other Silesian and German factories did use similar finishes and decorations. Thus in this section the problems discussed are basically those connected with the RSP Red Mark.

Reproductions

A reproduction is a problem that results when any item suddenly is in great demand, becomes scarce, and has a high price (whenever it is available). RSP porcelain fits this description. Since the 1960s, RSP collecting has been growing rapidly. Interest and activity in this field has reached a high level. It is not surprising, therefore, that for the last several years, attempts to copy RSP in various ways have been evident.

A true reproduction copies an item exactly without trying to deceive. Fake copies are items which are exactly the same as the genuine article and which are intended to deceive. RSP reproductions actually fall somewhere in between these terms. There is a "fake" RSP Red Mark available today. This mark comes in the form of a decal which can be applied, glazed, and fired onto a piece of procelain. This particular fake mark has been seen on "unmarked" RSP, new porcelain with RSP type decor, new porcelain with RSP type molds, and on other unmarked "old" 19th century porcelain.

The mark itself is a very good representation of the authentic mark (see Plate R1). Upon close inspection, however, there are some discrepancies. The "i" in Prussia is not dotted and there is no period after Prussia. It is true that these parts could be missing from genuine RSP marks because the original marks were placed over the glaze rather than under the glaze (see Section 2); and wear could have obliterated parts of the mark. A better indication that the mark is a fake is that the leaves in the wreath are shaped too perfectly, the green is not the right color, and the "a" in Prussia is filled in (note the genuine mark, Plate 4). The mark has a new look overall compared to the old, but it is easy at first glance to mistake the mark for the real thing—that is its purpose!

New pieces of porcelain are imported from Japan today which attempt to resemble RSP in type, decor, and even mold. Such pieces may be unmarked or marked with a red wreath and star and the initials R.S., or by a green wreath and star without the initials (see Plates R2, R3, and R4). A paper label with "Made in Japan" is usually on the pieces. The label, of course, is easy to remove. These pieces are decorated with floral designs and new transfers. Some of the transfers have the same or similar themes as those seen on RSP. The "Melon Eaters" and a pastoral scene (even "signed" Boucher) are examples. Portrait themes of a Victorian type girl are also the decoration on several objects.

All types of items are manufactured (for a few pictures see Plates R5 to R14). The shoe, small ewer, and covered candy dish are mold copies of RSP. Other items may have a long bar (stress mark) as part of the mold on the bottom. Many people think that such a mark denotes a piece as "very old." These pieces of porcelain do not in any way compare to the standards of RSP items. That they are not genuine is usually quite apparent to an experienced collector, but not always to the new collector. (I have in fact had one beginner to ask me how I could tell the difference, because to her the "new" was really prettier than the "old." Needless to say, that person should not start collecting RSP until she has studied the topic much more thoroughly.)

The new porcelain is fairly thick. The attempts at scalloping, scroll designs, and lattice work are clumsy, rather than delicate in appearance. The decoration is too bright, and the backgrounds are not subtle. The transfers are often poorly applied. The gold trim does not have the patina or burnished look of the original pieces. This trim is sometimes uneven, evidently applied hastily and not by an expert. Some of the objects, to my knowledge, were never made as RSP items—the two part egg, large jewelry box, or *metal* handled cracker jar, for example. Such pieces are reproductions that are misleading by their shape, decor, and mark (if marked). They are not truly fakes. The exact mark of R.S. Prussia is not copied. Similar items, however, have Nippon or Occupied Japan marks. These items so marked are more misleading than those items with the R.S. wreath mark. Although, like the RSP type items, it is clear to experienced collectors that the pieces are not genuine Nippon or Occupied Japan articles, the marks say that they are. Nippon and Occupied Japan are place names, however, and not factory marks like the RSP mark.

The manufacturer or importer of these types of items does not sell the pieces as the genuine article. The prices attest to this—they are quite inexpensive. Many of these pieces are sold in gift shops and at flea markets. The retail prices are also inexpensive compared to today's RSP prices. Most of the items retail from $12 to $35, although the jewelry box, or a portrait tankard may be $65 or more. These prices should alert the buyer. There are few sellers who are unaware of the market price of RSP, and there are few, if any, bargains today in this field of collecting. A small ewer priced at $12 or $15 is obviously not genuine when the authentic item commands a figure forty or more times that amount.

Some people, however, are placing the fake RSP mark on some of these new items. In some cases, they are trying to sell the pieces for the same prices that the genuine RSP items command. This type of practice is the real problem.

Some other new porcelain, different in type of object and decor from those described above, has recently been seen with the fake RSP mark (see Plates R15, R16 and R17). The china is of fair quality, but it is not old. The pieces are relatively plain in shape. The gold trim is too bright, and the floral decoration is not very distinctive as an RSP type of decoration. Again, the prices are too cheap.

Dorothy Hammond in *Confusing Collectables* notes that the Lefton China Company marketed some years ago pieces of porcelain which had an R.S. Prussia mark. She notes that Prussia, however, was spelled with one "s". Thus this type of spelling should immediately alert the buyer to the fact that the piece is a misleading reproduction.

A more serious problem than these "reproduced" items or the fake mark on these new items is when an *unmarked* but actually authentic (see Unmarked RSP in this section) piece of RSP has the fake mark put on it. Hoping to get a better price, an overzealous seller may do this. At whatever point in time the fake mark is discovered, the piece and its price will be discredited. This fake mark can, of course, be applied to any type of porcelain—new porcelain, unmarked RSP, or any genuinely "old" unmarked porcelain of any origin. Due to the variety of types of RSP items and decoration subjects, an uninformed buyer might easily be cheated in this way. Because of such practices, some people have told me that they are "afraid" of RSP in general. If buyers are fully aware of these deceptive practices and knowledgeable about genuine RSP, they really do not have to be "afraid"—only informed and careful.

In Section 2, I wrote that some of the RSP marks were green or that the colors in the wreath and lettering might vary from the Red Mark. Such marks appear to be due to a faulty or uneven firing process. The marks do not appear to be "fakes." Certainly mistakes in marking at the factory would occur occasionally. Although molds can be duplicated and decorations imitated, there was absolutely no reason for other companies to copy RSP products during the time they were manufactured. Other companies would not have any reason to put a mark resembling the RSP mark on their products. RSP porcelain items were not more expensive than other porcelain products at that time. Moreover, there was a large enough export market available to accommodate the production of many factories.

And, finally, no one then could suspect that in the 1970s and 1980s RSP would be such a desirable acquisition. Pieces seen with RSP marks which vary in color from the red mark appear to be from the same time period as the red marked items. The pieces also seem to exemplify the same type of mold shape and decoration characteristics of other red marked RSP items.

As is clear by the current attempts at RSP reproductions or new "Prussia" type pieces, it is impossible to reproduce all of the RSP characteristics. A piece which has only one or two of these characteristics will not convince knowledgeable buyers that it is the genuine article. But attempts will continue to be made, and some buyers will ultimately be cheated.

Altered or Repaired RSP

A question that concerns many collectors and dealers as much as reproductions and fake marks, is the problem of repaired or altered pieces. China making and decorating have staged a comeback in recent years. Many people have a talent for this type of art. Also advanced technology and new methods and materials make mending and decorating easier today. Amateur mending is usually quite obvious, but today there are specialists around the country who restore RSP specifically as well as other porcelain items. A broken piece can be put back together, chips can be repaired, and handles, finials, lids, and legs can be mended or *remade*. Restoring means to return something to its original condition. This can be accomplished by putting broken parts back together or by *making* a new part when the old part is missing or too badly broken to be mended. These new parts really alter the piece. With new parts, the piece may look the same, but it is not the same as the original.

Gold trim, gold stenciled designs, and colored glazes can be accomplished by professional restorers. Professional artists can also add new decoration—an animal, for instance—to old pieces. New decoration can be handpainted on pieces that may have an undecorated area. The work may fit in nicely; it may even add to the piece; but it is altered nonetheless. The buyer must learn to identify handpainted work (see Section 2).

Repairs and restoration by professionals are usually invisible to the naked eye. Pieces must be scrutinized carefully or viewed under a black light which will show where the piece has been mended. Some restorers, though, even advertise that their repairs resist the black light test. Of course, it is not wrong to repair or restore a piece of porcelain. Mended porcelain has been common through the ages. Museums exhibit many repaired or even badly broken examples—because they are rarities. Individuals often repair items or have them professionally repaired for sentimental reasons, or because they really want to use the item, or they need it to complete their collection. That is not the problem; rather the problem is only when such repaired or altered items are sold to buyers under the guise that they have *not* been mended or that new parts or new decoration have *not* been added. The restorers may not practice such deception, but it may be practiced by people who have items repaired. The expense involved is really not great compared to the price that can be obtained if the item is presented as original in mint condition. (Pieces which are even chipped, or missing a part, if they have the RSP mark, still have quite a value to collectors as is evident from prices paid at auction for such pieces. This is not true for most other porcelain products manufactured by other companies during the same era.) Pieces that are advertised as repaired or altered do not bring the same prices as those in perfect condition. This is also evident at auction. If a purchased piece is found to have some damage or repair not explicitly noted by the auctioneer, the piece is quickly returned by the buyer to be reauctioned. The same buyer often is the ultimate buyer—but at a lower price. It is only fair that damaged or repaired pieces should cost less than ones in good and original condition. One might say, "Well, if the repairs are not visible, what difference does it make?" The difference is that a price is being paid for something that it is not. It comes down, of course, to morals and ethics.

As a rule of thumb, all RSP pieces should be examined closely in a good light (if not a black light). The buyer should also routinely check for hairlines, flakes, and chips. It is very easy, even for experienced collectors and dealers, to miss small flaws—until perhaps much later. Porcelain should have a bell-like sound when tapped gently. Check this quality. If there is a dullness, look for the imperfection.

Double Marks and Mold Marks

Double marks and mold marks are often confusing. Double marks refer to a genuine RSP mark, plus some other mark, on the back of an object. In many instances the double mark on RSP items is the factory "Handpainted" mark, or Reinhold's script marks (see Plates 6 to 9). A department store name may accompany the RSP mark in some instances. These types of double marks are usually straightforward and unambiguous.

Sometimes though the RSP mark (or other R.S. and E.S. marks) is accompanied by a beehive mark or a Royal Vienna mark (see Plates 15 and 16). Some references note that a beehive mark like the one in Plate 16 was used by the Suhl factory. However beehive marks were used by many 19th century porcelain manufacturers and decorators. Pieces which have this mark in addition to a Suhl factory mark are often decorated with classical or mythological decor. That particular type of decor is reminiscent of decorated porcelain from the 18th century Vienna factory. I suggest that the beehive mark might have been used by the Suhl factory to denote that particular form of decoration. Alternatively, other European companies or decorators could have purchased Suhl factory blanks and added the beehive mark. The Royal Vienna mark in Plate 15 definitely appears to be that of a late 19th or early 20th century decorating company. Other pieces, with other manufacturer's marks and "Royal Vienna" as well as "Royal Vienna" alone are seen on various porcelain examples. It is incorrect to attribute such pieces which have only the Royal Vienna mark (not accompanied by an R.S. or E.S. mark) to the Suhl factory. In my opinion these marks are similar to the Pickard mark which is often on pieces with an RSG mark (see Section 3). The Pickard mark alone definitely does not indicate that the porcelain piece came from the Tillowitz factory.

Marks made as a part of the mold—a raised star, a raised cross, a raised diamond shape, or a raised circle (see

Plates 10 to 14) are another problem. Many people attribute any piece of porcelain marked in one of these ways as RSP. They do this because the RSP mark has been seen in conjunction with these marks on some pieces. Reliable references, however, do not show these types of marks as factory marks of either the Suhl or Tillowitz factory.

The raised star, especially, is thought by some collectors to be the oldest RSP mark. Research shows that the Wallendorf factory in Thuringia (Erdmann's Suhl factory, as you recall, was also located in Thuringia) used a "star" mark during the 1760s. It is evident that the examples which do have a raised star mark did not come from that era. Because a printed star is part of the RSP mark, it is conceivable that a molded star might have been used in the early days of the factory, but the date cannot be authenticated. Other factory marks are also seen in conjunction with a molded star mark, the Royal Rudolstadt mark for example. As it was a common practice for porcelain companies to decorate wares of other companies before they were producing porcelain themselves, it is possible that the blanks with the raised star mold marks were made elsewhere and decorated by one of the Schlegelmilch factories. Few pieces are seen with the "raised star" mold mark. This scarcity of examples might imply that the marks were used prior to the RSP mark and the peak exporting period of the company. When a piece has both a mold mark and the RSP mark, there is no question that the piece was at least decorated, if not manufactured, at the Suhl or Tillowitz factory. If the mold matches an RSP marked mold exactly, it is also probable, even without an RSP mark, that the piece is a Suhl or Tillowitz factory made item.

Sometimes, though, there are examples of molds which do not match exactly an RSP marked mold. These examples are unmarked except for one of the mold marks. The mold itself may have all of the RSP characteristics according to decoration and ornate shape, except an RSP mark. Because of the popularity of some these "mold marked only" pieces by collectors, I have included some examples in the RSP mold identification system and photographs. I hope that readers will let me know and send photographs of the object and the mark if they have double marked examples (mold mark with RSP mark).

The raised circle mold mark especially could have been used by other factories. Stress marks alone (long raised bar shapes) certainly do not identify an RSP item. These marks and ridges were necessary to add strength to the piece when it was fired. Many companies used them then, and some still do. (Note that some of the reproductions also have mold stress marks.)

Any piece of porcelain—unmarked, stress marked, raised marked, or factory stamped—should be judged on its merits: the quality of the porcelain, the quality of the decoration, and most importantly, the desire of the buyer. One must determine ultimately whether one is collecting only for enjoyment, only for profit, or for both, and judge the pieces one buys accordingly.

Other Prussia Marks

The word "Prussia," as part of a mark, does not mean that the piece was made by one of the Schlegelmilch factories, just as the name "Limoges" in a mark does not mean that the piece was made by the Haviland factory. Both "Prussia" and "Limoges" are names that denote a geographical location, not the name of a company! Many factories were operating at the same time in both Prussia and Limoges. Some of the factories were larger and better known than others. The factories were located in these areas because the necessary ingredients for making porcelain were also located in those areas. Porcelain products from any of the companies in the same area would be of a comparable quality in most instances. The types of items produced and their shapes and decoration might be different, but often they were also similar.

The Royal Rudolstadt mark is probably the other (than RSP) most commonly seen Prussia mark. This mark was used by Beyer and Boch. Their company was located in Volkstedt which, like Suhl, was in the Thuringia region of Prussia. The company was a decorating firm in the 1850s and did not begin producing procelain until the 1890s. Many of the products are similar to RSP items. The mark for the company was composed of the letter "B" in a semi-shield with a crown and Prussia above the Royal Rudolstadt below, all in green.

Some other "Prussia" marks include the Wheelock Trademark of a wheel and lock in red and green and Prussia below in red. A red half-man, half-lion figure with Prussia in a lozenge underneath is the same mark (without the word "Prussia" in it) that is attributed to P. Donath, a porcelain manufacturer in lower Silesia from circa 1882 to 1933. A green clover leaf with C.S. Prussia below, and a blue S. and E. monogram with 1811 inside and Prussia spelled with a German "S" are other marks occasionally found on porcelain items. There is even less historical information concerning these companies and their marks than there is about the Schlegelmilch factories. Probably they were very small concerns. Examples with these marks are not seen too frequently compared to the amount of pieces with RSP marks. Pieces so marked should not cause confusion with RSP for the pieces are accurately marked as another Prussian factory product. Such pieces should be collectable in their own right.

Unmarked RSP

Not all RSP products were marked. Some people are skeptical about this fact, but study and evidence supports the claim. A reasonable question is: "If the porcelain does not have a back mark, how can one know that it is in fact an RSP item?" Many examples of European porcelain from the late 1800s to the early 1900s were quite similar in form and decoration. It is not easy to attribute many unmarked pieces to any particular factory or even to any specific country of origin. RSP porcelain, however, has a distinct advantage. Because of its many unique characteristics, which in turn give the porcelain a distinct image, many unmarked pieces can be verified as RSP. There are too many unmarked pieces which match exactly not only the mold but also the decor of marked pieces. It is clear that such pieces were made by the same factory.

Several reasons can be given to explain the unmarked examples. First, the companies were not required by law (European export law or American import law) to mark every piece. Second, at the peak of the export demand, it would have been simpler to leave off the mark. A back mark not only identifies a company, but also serves as proof of quality. That is probably why so many pieces were marked. But the stores that were retailing or wholesaling the wares in this country were not concerned that every piece be marked. They were interested in obtaining the merchandise as soon as possible. (Remember the pieces had to come by sea which took considerable time.) Thus marks of the manufacturer on part of a set or part of a line could suffice. Buyers were primarily interested in attractive but affordable pieces to decorate their home and table—back marks were secondary. They also did not realize that they were purchasing future antiques! Third, errors of course, could have occurred at the factory. It would be possible for some pieces to slip by occasionally and be exported without the mark. It is not unusual to see a piece with a whole RSP mark and part of a mark —an obvious marking error.

Although "blanks" could have been made by other factories in similar mold forms during the same time period, or even today for that matter, the combination of decorations and finishes typical of RSP items would almost defy exact replication. Most importantly, such blanks would usually have had handpainted decoration. It appears that RSP factory handpainted items were marked with the RSP mark and a "Handpainted" mark (see Plate 6). So if unmarked examples have handpainted decoration, it is almost certain that such pieces were not decorated at the factory.

If new transfers are seen on unmarked porcelain, it is quite apparent that not only are the transfers new, but that the porcelain is also new. New transfers of the "Melon Eaters" are immediately recognized as new products when compared to RSP items with this type of decoration.

Advanced collectors really seem to have no qualms in purchasing "unmarked" RSP items, especially if the mold is the same as that of a marked piece. The more simple the mold, the more difficult it becomes to attribute the piece as RSP. Some criteria can be established for determining unmarked pieces as RSP items:

(1) If the unmarked piece is exactly like a marked piece in its mold shape and decoration; or

(2) If the unmarked piece is in the same or matching mold of a marked example although the decoration is not the same but has RSP characteristics—same type of decoration subjects and finishes as other marked RSP items.

(3) If an unmarked piece does not match a mold of a marked piece, but the mold is ornate and the decoration is ornate with RSP type subjects and finishes, the probability is high that it is an RSP piece, though less certain than items falling into categories 1 and 2.

(4) Unmarked pieces which are simply molded, unless they match exactly an RSP marked item both in mold and decoration (like in criterion 1) are more difficult to attribute as RSP.

In the section on Mold Identification, each mold pictured that has been seen both marked and unmarked is noted. Molds that fit criterion 3 are included in the Mold ID system, but I note that they have been seen only as unmarked examples. Items fitting criterion 4 are not included. When identically marked and unmarked pieces can be matched as to mold and decoration, or just to ornate mold with RSP type decoration, price differentials appear only slightly to favor the marked objects.

5.
Collecting Trends

RSP porcelain is really a collector's delight. It meets the criteria for an antique and collectable object. Pieces are over 50 years old, and earlier ones are 100 years old or close to that age. A large amount of these items was exported to this country and to Canada during the early part of this century. As a result, until recently, there has been a good supply on the market for collectors. But, since the companies stopped production many years ago, there is definitely a finite amount, so scarcity also makes it attractive. Finally, RSP has an excellent inherent facility for being collected.

Any attempt to work out special types of collections leads one to imagine numerous, rich, and varied prospects. Because many pieces were made from the same or matching molds, specific molds can be collected. As most of the decorative subjects were applied by transfer, and thus the same decoration was applied to so many objects, collections can consist of just one particular subject, or one can collect as many of the decorative themes and subjects as possible. For example, someone might want only pieces with Lebrun's self portrait, or only pieces decorated with roses. Others might want animal examples of any type or any kind of scenic theme. Some might desire only pieces with a satin finish. Or as is probably most frequently the case, collectors collect all types of pieces with all types of decoration.

The RSP handpainted pieces, though few in number, present an interesting category for collections. Because they are scarce, it would be difficult to acquire a large collection consisting only of handpainted pieces. Individual handpainted examples, however, are usually welcome additions to collections. A totally handpainted piece is inherently more valuable than pieces transfer decorated. They are usually one of a kind pieces (the same decoration could be handpainted on other pieces, of course). They do represent individual effort and creativity.

What is happening currently to the RSP market and what can one expect in the future? Judging by today's activity, it is clear that this category of porcelain will soon reach another cycle. Many of the most coveted pieces are held by advanced collectors. The prices of those items prohibit many collectors from adding to their collections. The consensus is that Animal themes are the most rare, hence they command the highest prices. The fruit themes are also scarce, but are not equally in demand or price to the animal pieces. Portrait, bird, and scenic themes are considered in the middle range. Many of these are also bringing good prices, but are still not approaching the prices of the animal decorated pieces. Floral themes are the least expensive because they are the most plentiful. Likewise bowls are the most common type of object and as a result bring less usually than other objects if they are floral decorated. The other themes of decoration on bowls will, of course, be in accordance with the price and popularity of the particular theme. However, the lowest prices of any piece—whatever its shape or decoration—today is comparable to the prices of the very best European antique porcelain.

Certain types of items which are scarce as well as certain molds are also of interest to collectors. The humidor is a rare type of porcelain item, as is the long spoonholder (see Plates 76 and 294). The carnation, iris, and ribbon and jewel molds are popular for their mold decoration. Items with a satin finish also rate high with collectors.

It is evident that as the most scarce and desirable items become difficult to find, the pieces with simpler molds or decoration will also rise in price. In such instances, the mark itself is the prime reason for its desirability. Today at shows, shops, or auctions, a single bowl—plainly molded and decorated, and once part of berry set—may bring a high figure, more than the whole berry set would have cost a few years ago.

Damaged pieces as well as repaired and restored items are also bought and sold for good sums. The decoration themes and types of items play a large part in the prices these damaged and repaired items bring. At a recent auction, a chocolate pot with a rim chip and a small hairline on the lip plus a chip on the rim of the lid brought $4400—it was decorated with a tiger and tigress, however. I have also seen a bread and butter plate broken into several pieces, badly and obviously mended which had a price tag of $75! Anyone who pays such a price does not have much of an investment!

Unmarked RSP is also gaining popularity and respect. Prices are becoming more comparable to marked pieces. Mold and decoration matches are helping to back up these pieces so that collectors no longer "shy" away from unmarked examples.

Some of the other marks, especially the steeple marks, are on fine pieces with ornate shapes and beautiful decoration. The cobalt pieces are quite outstanding. The Prov Saxe marks are on many examples decorated in the art nouveau style, and they are also quite desirable. The handpainted Prov Saxe, R.S. Germany, and R.S. Tillowitz marked items should gain popularity soon. Their prices would rise as a consequence. The art modern or art deco line often accentuates these pieces. As they do not have the RSP image, this might account for their being overlooked sometimes by collectors. The prices on such pieces are not yet equal to those of RSP, but this may change as collectors and dealers become more aware of the beauty of these hand decorated items. It is also probable that such pieces will gain favor with other porcelain collectors—collectors who do not collect RSP.

The R.S. Poland and R.S. Suhl wreath marks, due to their scarcity and to their similarity to the RSP mark are currently bringing good prices, more comparable to RSP than any other mark. This trend is expected to continue until prices do in fact equal those of RSP.

R.S. Germany items that are in the same or similar mold forms as RSP items are, of course, bringing prices comparable to RSP. Some other RSG items, though are also desirable: for example, the handpainted pieces and those with outstanding transfer decorations like the Sheepherder. The majority of RSG marked items are table ware items rather than art objects. Such pieces are less in demand unless a whole set of some particular pattern can be collected. Some of the table wares that are fashioned along ultra modern lines are quite attractive, and interest in these pieces should increase. Other examples are plain and are really exactly what they were meant to be—dishes for eating. It is unlikely that these plain pieces will ever reach the prices of RSP items. Prices, in general though, on RSG pieces, even blanks, are increasing. Again some sellers are taking advantage of the "R.S." mark. High prices can be seen on some very plain pieces. Just because the piece has an RSG mark does not make it necessarily rare or desirable—any more so than any other European porcelain of a similar vintage. There are simply too many pieces of these types on the market. The RSG items should be judged according to their artistic qualities. There are still plenty of these around for the dedicated and serious collector.

At present there are few collectors concentrating solely on R.S. Germany marked pieces. Desirable pieces with this mark are added to RSP or other porcelain collections. Likewise, RSG blanks decorated by Pickard or other professional decorating studios are collectable of course, not just for the RSG mark, but for the unique handpainted decoration.

As the prices have risen so drastically in the past few years for RSP, many dealers as well as collectors have turned their attention to these other R.S. and E.S. marks. Being alert to the choice pieces may well pay off in the future.

Also of interest to collectors and dealers are the many other lovely porcelain pieces on the market with other German, Austrian, and Silesian marks. One should be informed about these other marks and the types of porcelain with such marks. Many are beautiful pieces and handsomely decorated. Some have finishes and decorative themes similar to RSP. But, on the whole, prices are still quite reasonable. Who knows which of these may soon become the next "R.S. Prussia?"

6.
RSP Mold Identification and Numbering System

Many dealers and collectors have said they need a system for quick identification and reference to the many RSP molds. An RSP mold identification system is useful for advertising pieces to sell when photographs are not always available—through trade papers, by telephone, and auction listings, for example. Identifying the various themes and subjects of decoration, as well as the finishes and trims, is more straightforward and concise than describing molds. By looking at a piece one can say that it is decorated with swans, flowers, or a cottage scene; however, advertising a bowl with a Lebrun portrait cannot identify what kind of a bowl it is. Different bowl molds may have the same Lebrun (or any other decoration theme) subject. A detailed word description of the mold not only can be lengthy but also unclear. It is easier to have a specific number to identify a specific mold. Because of the variety and number of RSP molds, such a task seems almost impossible. One can look at a large collection, and it seems that each piece represents a different mold. In fact, I was convinced after studying hundreds of pictures of individual pieces, that when I did try to match molds, I would have at least nearly as many different molds as I did pictures! Happily, that was not the case. It is really fascinating to see how many identical or matching molds were produced, but decorated in a variety of ways. The decoration in many instances often makes it difficult to see that one mold is the same as another.

All RSP molds are not presented, of course, in this edition. Also the Mold ID system is just for R.S. Prussia objects. Other R.S. or E.S. marked pieces are not included in the mold ID system. Some popular "unmarked" examples which are attributed by collectors to R.S. Prussia, however, are included in the RSP mold descriptions. Such examples are noted as "unmarked" in their photograph captions. Also if a pictured RSP marked mold has been seen and authenticated (through actual examination) in unmarked examples, that information is noted with the mold description of the RSP marked item. All molds shown have the RSP RED MARK unless stated to the contrary in their photograph captions.

I have assigned a mold number to each photograph of each RSP object. Because some molds have such outstanding characteristics, specific names are commonly associated with some molds. Such examples have a name as well as a mold number. There are relatively few molds, however, that suggest obvious names. Thus, I decided to give only a number to the majority of the molds. Names are helpful, but because so many different molds exist, creating labels for them can develop quickly into names which may not identify precisely the mold characteristics.

To make the system easy to use and as simple as possible, I divided the RSP molds into four categories by types of objects.

(1) *Flat or round* objects—bowls, plates, trays, celery and relish dishes—comprise category 1. This category groups molds of these objects by (a) popular name such as "icicle" or "carnation"; (b) unusual body shape such as blown out concave sections, dome shapes or star shapes; or (c) border characteristics such as pointed, scalloped, scrolled, or smooth.

(2) *Vertical or tall* objects—coffee, tea, chocolate pots, tankards, pitchers, cups, biscuit jars, sugars, creamers—comprise category 2. This category groups molds of these objects according to the type of *base* of the object: (a) flat, (b) scalloped; (c) elevated scalloped, (d) pedestal foot; (e) molded feet, or (f) applied feet.

(3) Accessory Items—hatpin holders, hair receivers, talcum shakers, pin boxes, candleholders, muffineers—comprise category 3. This category groups molds just according to *type* of object.

(4) Ferners and Vases comprise category 4. This category groups molds also according to *type* of object.

Within these four categories, pieces with the same mold are shown together and have the same mold number. Of course a bowl and a plate or a tray would not have been made from the same mold but in *matching* molds. Such matching molds, however, are identified by the same mold number. Sometimes, though, many of the Flat objects in Category 1 have matching molds in Category 2, Vertical objects. Many RSP pieces were made in matching sets. If there is a chocolate pot, there is probably also a cake plate in the same mold as well as other vertical pieces like cups, creamer, sugar, and biscuit jar. In such instances where a particular mold is shown in more than one category, the number of the mold will be different for each category, but the reader will be cross referenced to the other categories. Molds with popular names keep the same names in each category but have a different Mold Number.

Just as it was not possible to show every known RSP mold in this edition, it was not possible to show an example of each piece that was made in the same or matching molds. Thus, if you have a plate, for example, that matches the mold of a bowl shown—but your plate is not shown—simply use the same Mold Number as that assigned to the bowl. Where possible, different objects that have the same or matching mold are shown. Also, when available, the same molds with different decoration are shown to demonstrate how decoration can change the appearance of the mold. Ultimately the goal is to identify all RSP molds and show how many different items were made from the same or matching molds.

I have prepared a Mold Chart (see chart beginning on page 30) to use with the RSP photographs which are presented in the next section. The Chart is divided into the four general categories of Molds. Each Mold Category is subdivided according to the specific characteristics of the molds. Molds with common characteristics (flat objects with scalloped borders, for example) are grouped together and if necessary the common characteristic is further broken down (flat objects with scalloped borders will be classified according to type of scallop— round, crimped, wavy, and so forth).

Each of the four basic categories of types of objects (Flat, Vertical, Accessory, Vases) has a set of numbers which identifies molds in those categories. Unused numbers are left at the end of each general Mold Type in all four categories in order to have adequate space to assign Mold Numbers to future RSP items as they are photographed and classified according to Mold. Thus, in Category 1, Popular Named Molds start with Mold Number 1 and actually go to Number 31, but the next Set of Numbers for Floral Border Shapes starts with Mold Number 51 instead of 32.

R.S. Prussia Mold Identification Chart

Category 1—Flat or Round Objects

Mold Numbers	Photo Numbers	Type of Mold	General Characteristics
1-50	35-108	Popular Named Molds (Iris, etc.)	A particular feature in the body or the border of the mold suggests an obvious mold name.
51-75	109-118	Floral Border Molds	The border of the mold is composed of floral designs usually separated by other shapes such as scallops or points. The floral designs are not always easy to see at first glance.
76-150	119-159	Unusual Body Shape	The body of the mold is composed of blown out sections usually in the form of dome or star shapes.
151-180	160-171	Pointed Border Molds	The overall border design is pointed. There may be notched indentations between the points. Such molds must be easily distinguishable from scalloped molds and have no rounded sides.
181-200	172-177	Rounded Scalloped Border	Border has rounded scallop sections of equal size. The sections may be beaded or fluted.
201-250	178-200	Semi-Round Scalloped Border	The scallop sections are not perfectly round. There may be a slight indentation or some other configuration between the scallops. The edges of the scallops can be smooth, beaded, or fluted.
251-275	201-218	Crimped Scalloped Border	Scallop sections are pinched or indented.
276-299	219-223	Wavy Scalloped Border	The scallop sections resemble a wavy line with a slight rounded center and shallow indentations on each side. The wavy sections may be separated by other small configurations such as scroll designs or points.
300-325	224-235	Elongated Scalloped Border	The scallop sections are long rather than round. The center of the section has either a slight indentation, or a sharp rounded point. The elongated scallops may be separated by other small configurations.
326-400	236-261	Irregular Scalloped Borders	Borders are composed of more than one of the above kind of scallops or some other configuration such as a point or scroll design. These molds are usually quite elaborate.
401-425	262-269	Scrolled Borders	Border is composed of ornate, curving scallop designs not only on the border but extending into the body of the object.
426-450	270-273	Smooth Borders	Border is completely smooth. The overall shape of the object may vary: round, oval, or rectangular.

Category 2—Vertical or Tall Objects

Mold Numbers	Photo Numbers	Type of Mold	General Characteristics
451-500	274-294	Smooth Bases	Base of object is perfectly level or flat on the bottom.
501-575	295-353	Flat Scalloped Base	The border of the base of the object is scalloped, but there is no elevation.
576-600	354-361	Elevated Scalloped Base	The base of the object has a scalloped border composed of equal or varied sized scallops. Indentations between the scallops elevate the object slightly.
601-625	362-373	Pedestal Foot	Objects may have a long or a short pedestal base. Long pedestals have a stem section between the base and body; short pedestals have no stem section. The bases of the pedestals may be round, square, smooth, or scalloped.
626-700	374-415	Molded Feet	Feet for the object are shaped as part of the body mold.
701-725	416-422	Applied Feet	Definite feet are applied to the base of the object.

Category 3—Accessory Items

Mold Numbers	Photo Numbers	Type of Mold	
726-750	423-427	Hatpin Holders	
751-775	428-429	Muffineers	
776-800	430	Talcum Shakers	
801-825	431-436	Hair Receivers	
826-850	437	Pin Boxes	
851-875	438	Candleholders	

Category 4—Ferners and Vases

Mold Numbers	Photo Numbers	Type of Mold	
876-899	439-442	Ferners	
900-950	443-455	Vases	

7.
Suggested Chronology of R.S. and E.S. Schlegelmilch Marks

Marks 1, 2, and 3	Steeple Marks Prussia and Germany attributed to Reinhold Schlegelmilch's Tillowitz, Silesia Factory	circa mid 1870s to 1880
Marks 4, 5, and 6	R.S. Prussia Marks attributed to either the Suhl or Tillowitz Factories	circa late 1870s to 1914 for the R.S. Prussia Marks
Marks 7, 8, and 9	R.S. Prussia Marks with R.S. Germany Mark, attributed to Reinhold Schlegelmilch's Tillowitz Factory	
Marks 10, 11, and 12 Marks 13, 14, and 15 Marks 16 to 23	R.S. Prussia Mark with mold marks Mold marks only Marks attributed to Erdmann Schlegelmilch's Suhl Factory	circa 1900 to mid 1920s
Marks 24 to 29	R.S. Germany Marks attributed to Reinhold's Schlegelmilch's Tillowitz, Silesia Factory	circa 1910 to 1956
Marks 30, 31, and 32	R.S. Tillowitz and R.S. Silesia Marks attributed to Reinhold Schlegelmilch's Tillowitz, Silesia Factory	circa 1920 to mid 1930s
Marks 33 and 34	R.S. Poland Mark attributed to Reinhold Schlegelmilch's Tillowitz, Silesia Factory	circa 1945 to 1956

Marks

PLATE 1, MARK 1. red, Tillowitz.

PLATE 2, MARK 2. dark green, Tillowitz.

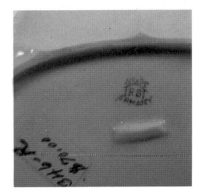

PLATE 3, MARK 3. red, Tillowitz.

PLATE 4, MARK 4. red, Suhl or Tillowitz.

PLATE 5, MARK 5. green, Suhl or Tillowitz.

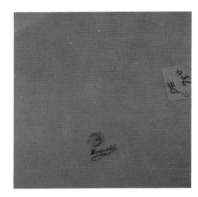

PLATE 6, MARK 6. red with gold "Handpainted," Suhl or Tillowitz.

PLATE 7, MARK 7. green RSP with red RSG, Tillowitz.

PLATE 8, MARK 8. red RSP, red RSG, Tillowitz.

PLATE 9, MARK 9. red RSP, gold RSG, Tillowitz.

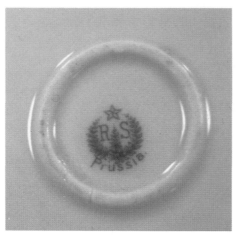

PLATE 10, MARK 10. red RSP, Suhl or Tillowitz, with mold mark.

PLATE 11, MARK 11. red RSP, Suhl or Tillowitz, with mold mark.

PLATE 12, MARK 12. mold mark, origin undetermined.

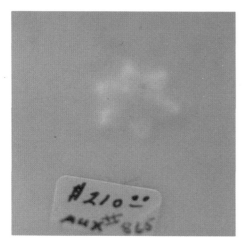

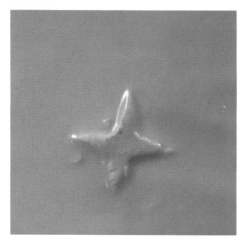

PLATE 13, MARK 13. mold mark, origin undetermined.

PLATE 14, MARK 14. mold mark, origin undetermined.

PLATE 15, MARK 15. red RSP, Suhl or Tillowitz, with gold Royal Vienna Mark.

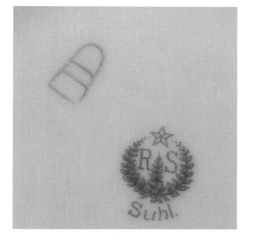

PLATE 16, MARK 16. red (or green not pictured), Suhl, with or without blue beehive.

PLATE 17, MARK 17. red, Suhl.

PLATE 18, MARK 18. blue-green, Suhl.

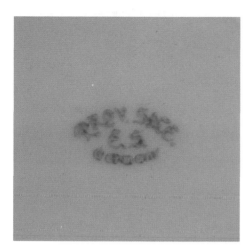

PLATE 19, MARK 19. green, Suhl.

PLATE 20, MARK 20. green, Suhl.

PLATE 21, MARK 21. green, Suhl.

PLATE 22, MARK 22. green, Suhl.

PLATE 23, MARK 23. green, Suhl.

PLATE 24, MARK 24. blue RSG with red script, Tillowitz.

PLATE 25, MARK 25. blue RSG, Tillowitz.

PLATE 26, MARK 26. green RSG, Tillowitz.

PLATE 27, MARK 27. green RSG, Tillowitz.

PLATE 28, MARK 28. green RSG (with or without "Handpainted"), Tillowitz.

PLATE 29, MARK 29. gold "Handpainted" RSG, Tillowitz.

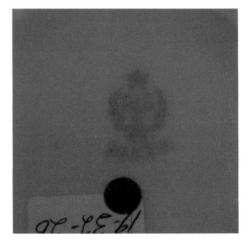

PLATE 30, MARK 30. blue R. S. Tillowitz (with or without Silesia, Germany, or "Handpainted"), Tillowitz.

PLATE 31, MARK 31. green or blue R. S. Silesia, Tillowitz.

PLATE 32, MARK 32. uncolored R. S. Silesia, Tillowitz.

PLATE 33, MARK 33. red R. S. Poland with blue RSG and gold "Handpainted," Tillowitz.

PLATE 34, MARK 34. red R. S. Poland (with or without "Germany" or "Handpainted"), Tillowitz.

R. S. Prussia Molds and Photographs*
Popular Named Molds (Plates 35 to 108)

PLATE 35, MOLD 1. "Acorn or Nut" Mold. Bowl, 10″d, satin finish.

PLATE 36, MOLD 2. "Grape and Leaf" Mold. Bowl, 10″d, light tapestry finish on inner scroll designs.

PLATE 37, MOLD 3. "Heart" Mold. Bowl, 10″d, satin finish and stippled gold designs.

*All pieces shown are marked RSP unless otherwise indicated.

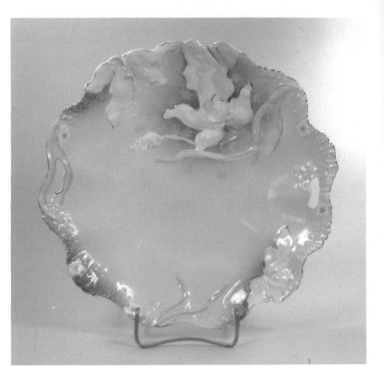

PLATE 38, MOLD 4. "Hidden Images" Mold. Bowl, 10″d, "Hidden Lady" on border, pearl finish, unmarked. Also see Plate 321 in Vertical Objects.

PLATE 39, MOLD 4. "Hidden Images" Mold. Cake Plate, 11″d, "Hidden Lady" on border, pearl finish, unmarked.

PLATE 40, MOLD 5. "Hidden Images" Mold. Cake Plate, 9½″d, "Hidden Lady" on border, pearl finish, unmarked. (Note "Hidden Lady" is different from Mold 4.)

PLATE 41, MOLD 6. "Hidden Images" Mold. Bowl, 10″d, "Hidden House" on border, pearl finish, unmarked.

PLATE 42, MOLD 7. "Icicle" Mold. Bowl, 11″d, Swans. See Plates 400 to 403 in Vertical Objects.

PLATE 43, MOLD 7. "Icicle" Mold. Bowl, 11″d, Barnyard animals with Pheasant.

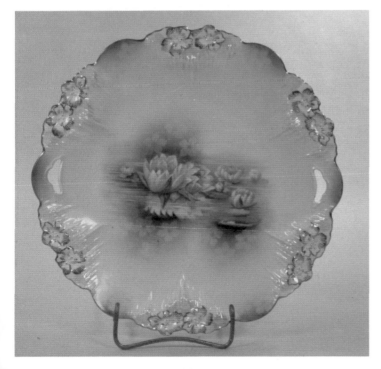

PLATE 44, MOLD 7. "Icicle" Mold. Cake Plate, 10″d, Reflecting Water Lilies.

PLATE 45, MOLD 8. "Icicle" Mold (Border variation). Bowl, 6″d, footed, Pheasant.

PLATE 46, MOLD 9. "Fleur-de-lys" Mold. Cake Plate, 10½"d, Summer portrait. Also see Plates 372 and 373 in Vertical Objects.

PLATE 47, MOLD 9. "Fleur-de-lys" Mold. Cake Plate, 12″d, Castle scene.

PLATE 48, MOLD 9. "Fleur-de-lys" Mold. Bowl, 10″d, Fruit decor.

PLATE 49, MOLD 9. "Fleur-de-lys" Mold. Bun Tray, 14″l.

PLATE 50, MOLD 10. "Leaf" Mold. Bowl, 9″l, 8″w, satin finish.

PLATE 51, MOLD 11. "Leaf Wreath" Mold. Bowl, 10½″d, Récamier portrait, iridescent Tiffany finish on deep leaf border, unmarked.

PLATE 52, MOLD 12. "Lettuce" Mold. Bowl, 9″d, pearl lustre finish.

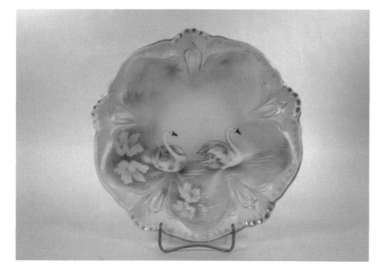

PLATE 53, MOLD 13. "Maize" Mold. Bowl, 10½″d, Swans, satin finish.

PLATE 54, MOLD 13. "Maize" Mold. Bowl, 10½″d.

PLATE 55, MOLD 14. "Medallion" Mold. Oblong Bowl, 13″l, 8½″w, Man in the Mountain scene, high glaze finish. Also see Plates 383 to 386 in Vertical Objects.

PLATE 56, MOLD 14. "Medallion" Mold. Celery, 14″l, 7″w, Reflecting poppies and daisies, portraits clockwise of Potocka, Lebrun, Récamier, Lebrun, tapestry finish on medallions.

PLATE 57, MOLD 14. "Medallion" Mold. Celery, 14″l, 7″w, Reflecting poppies and daisies, portraits of Diane the Huntress and Flora on each side.

PLATE 58, MOLD 14. "Medallion" Mold. Cake Plate, 11″d, portrait medallions (clockwise) Potocka, Lebrun, Lebrun, Lebrun, Récamier, Lebrun, tapestry finish on medallions, small Hanging Baskets around inside border.

PLATE 59, MOLD 14. "Medallion" Mold, Cake Plate, 10½"d, Sitting Basket, pearl lustre finish on outside border.

PLATE 60, MOLD 14. "Medallion" Mold. Bowl, 11"d, Sitting Basket, high glaze finish.

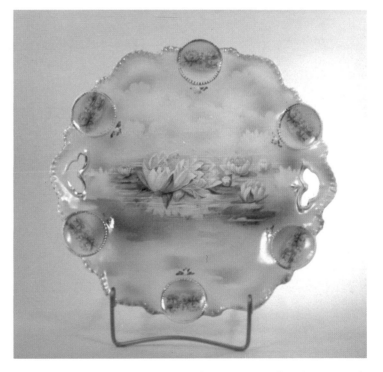

PLATE 61, MOLD 14. "Medallion" Mold. Bowl, 11"d, Man in the Mountain scene, high glaze finish. Unmarked.

PLATE 62, MOLD 14. "Medallion" Mold. Plate, 11"d, Reflecting water lilies. Unmarked.

PLATE 63, MOLD 15. "Pentagon" Mold. Bowl, 5½"d, 3 footed.

PLATE 64, MOLD 16. "Plume" Mold. Tray, 11½"l, 7½"w.

PLATE 65, MOLD 17. "Puff" Mold. Bowl, 10½d, footed, satin finish, mauve tones on outer border.

PLATE 66, MOLD 17. "Puff" Mold. Bowl, 10½d, satin finish, pale green tones on outer border.

PLATE 67, MOLD 17. "Puff" Mold. Bowl, 9½"d, pearlized finish, gold stippling and gold stencilled designs on inner border and between "Puff" sections.

PLATE 68, MOLD 18. "Ribbon and Jewel" Mold. Bowl, 11″d, Melon Eaters, gold stippled and stencilled decor, jewels decorated as opals. Unmarked examples also have been seen in this mold. Also see Plate 330 and 415 in Vertical Objects.

PLATE 69, MOLD 18. "Ribbon and Jewel" Mold. Bowl, 9″ Melon Eaters, gold stippled and stencilled decor, jewels decorated as opals. Note slight variation in decoration as compared to Plate 68.

PLATE 70, MOLD 18. "Ribbon and Jewel" Mold, Relish, 9½″l, 5″w, Lebrun portrait with gold stippled frame, jewels decorated as opals.

PLATE 71, MOLD 19. "Sea Creature" Mold. Bowl, 11″d, satin finish.

PLATE 72, MOLD 19. "Sea Creature" Mold. Bowl, 11″d, pearlized finish.

PLATE 73, MOLD 20. "Shell" Mold. Bowl, 11″l, 10″w, satin finish.

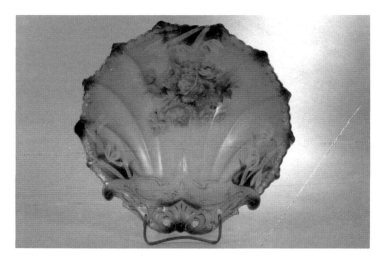

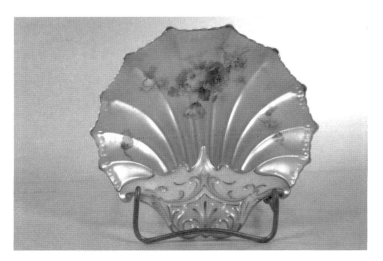

PLATE 74, MOLD 20. "Shell" Mold. Bowl, 11"l, 10"w, satin finish.

PLATE 75, MOLD 20. "Shell" Mold. Bowl, 6"l, 5½"w, satin finish.

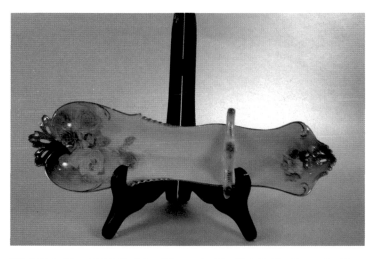

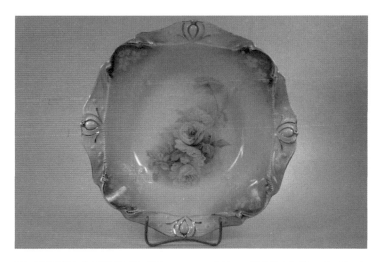

PLATE 76, MOLD 21. "Spoonholder" Mold. Spoonholder, 14"l.

PLATE 77, MOLD 22. "Square and Jewel" Mold. Bowl, 10"d, jewels on inner border.

PLATE 78, MOLD 23. "Stippled Floral" Mold. Plate, 8½″d, Winter portrait, gold stencilled inside border. Unmarked pieces also have been seen in this mold. Also see Plates 333 to 340 in Vertical Objects, and Plates 436 and 437 in Accessory Items.

PLATE 79, MOLD 23. "Stippled Floral" Mold. Celery, 12″l, 6″w, gold stencilled inside border.

PLATE 80, MOLD 23. "Stippled Floral" Mold. Cake Plate, 10″d, Lilies, unmarked.

PLATE 81, MOLD 23. "Stippled Floral" Mold. Tray, 11½″l, 7″w, gold stencilled designs inside border.

PLATE 82, MOLD 24. "Wheat Fleur-de-lys" Mold. Bowl, 10″d, Calla Lilies, pearlized finish.

Popular Named Floral Molds

PLATE 83, MOLD 25. "Iris" Mold. Bowl, 9½"d, Summer portrait, satin finish, on iris and border. Also see Plates 324, and 378 to 380 in Vertical Objects.

PLATE 84, MOLD 25. "Iris" Mold. Bowl, 10"d, Winter portrait, satin finish on iris and border.

PLATE 85, MOLD 25. "Iris" Mold. Relish, 9½"l, 4½"w, Winter portrait, satin finish on iris and border.

PLATE 86, MOLD 25. "Iris" Mold. Cake Plate, 11"d, Pink Poppies framed with gold stencilled floral design.

PLATE 87, MOLD 25. "Iris" Mold. Cake Plate, 10"d, gold on leaves.

PLATE 88, MOLD 26. "Iris Variation" Mold. Bowl, 10½"d, heavy gold border. Unmarked. Also see Plates 319 and 320 in Vertical Objects.

PLATE 89, MOLD 26. "Iris Variation" Mold. Dresser Tray, 11½"l, 7"w. Unmarked.

PLATE 90, MOLD 26. "Iris Variation" Mold. Bowl, 10"d. Unmarked.

PLATE 91, MOLD 26. "Iris Variation" Mold. Cake Plate, 11"d. Unmarked.

PLATE 92, MOLD 26. "Iris Variation" Mold. Bowl, 10½"d. Unmarked.

PLATE 93, MOLD 27. "Iris Variation" Mold. Bowl, 11"d, 4"h, rococo border with orchids in high relief, high glaze on outer border, pearl lustre finish on inner orchid border, gold stenciled designs inside border. Unmarked.

PLATE 94, MOLD 28. "Carnation" Mold. Centerpiece Bowl, 15"d, satin and pearlized finish, Pink Poppies. Also see Plates 325 and 341 to 351 in Vertical Objects.

PLATE 95, MOLD 28. "Carnation" Mold. Pair of Plates, 7½"d, watered silk bkgrd.

PLATE 96, MOLD 28. "Carnation" Mold. Bowl, 10½"d, pearlized finish on carnations, gold stippled frame around center rose decor.

PLATE 97, MOLD 28. "Carnation" Mold. Bowl, 10½"d, pearlized finish on carnations and border.

PLATE 98, MOLD 28. "Carnation" Mold. Tray, 11½"l, 7"w, pearlized and satin finish on carnations and border.

PLATE 99, MOLD 28. "Carnation" Mold. Berry Set, Master Bowl, 12"d, individual bowls (6), 6"d, pearlized and satin finish on carnations, gold outer border with inner gold stippled border.

PLATE 100, MOLD 29. "Lily" Mold. Bowl, 10″d, Récamier portrait, bronze iridescent Tiffany finish, gold stencilled inside border.

PLATE 101, MOLD 29. "Lily" Mold. Bowl, 10″d, Lebrun portrait, bronze iridescent Tiffany finish. Unmarked.

PLATE 102, MOLD 29. "Lily" Mold. Bowl, 10½″d. Unmarked except for "Germany."

PLATE 103, MOLD 29. "Lily" Mold. Oval Bowl, 13″l, 8½″w, Lebrun portrait, green iridescent Tiffany finish. Unmarked.

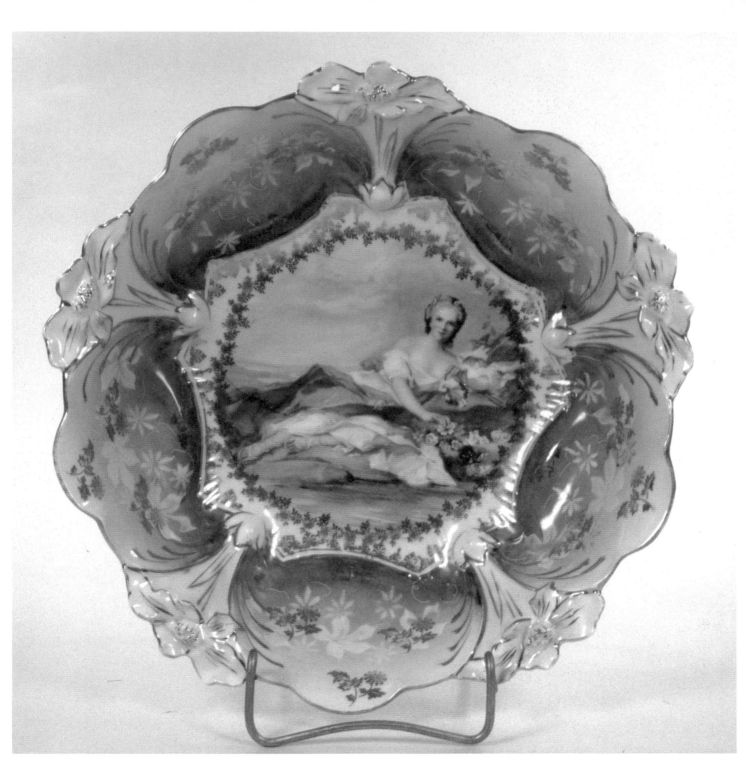

PLATE 104, MOLD 29. "Lily" Mold. Bowl, 10″d, Flora portrait, gold stencilled designs. Unmarked.

PLATE 105, MOLD 29. "Lily" Mold. Bowl, 10½"d, Potocka portrait. Unmarked.

PLATE 106, MOLD 30. "Lily" Mold. Bowl, 7"d, Récamier portrait. Note that mold is square with only 4 geometric shapes and the "lilies" are short stemmed. Unmarked.

PLATE 107, MOLD 31. "Sunflower" Mold. Bowl, 9½″d, satin finish. Also see Plates 293 and 374 in Vertical Objects.

PLATE 108, MOLD 31. "Sunflower" Mold. Bowl, 10½″d, white satin finish.

Floral Border Molds (Plates 109 to 118)

PLATE 109, MOLD 51. Cake Plate, 10½"d. Unmarked.

PLATE 110, MOLD 51. Cake Plate, 11"d, floral designs on border not decorated as flowers, some enamelling on floral decor, unmarked.

PLATE 111, MOLD 52. Bowl, 10½"d, pearl lustre border. Unmarked.

PLATE 112, MOLD 52. Bowl, 10½"d, pearl lustre border. Unmarked.

PLATE 113, MOLD 53. Bowl, 10"d, Reflecting water lilies.

PLATE 114, MOLD 53. Bowl, 10"d, Reflecting water lilies, green tones bkgrd.

PLATE 115, MOLD 54. Bowl, 10″d, high glaze on floral border shapes, unmarked.

PLATE 116, MOLD 55. Bowl, 10″d, Fruit decor.

PLATE 117, MOLD 56. Relish, 9½″l, 4½″w, cobalt iridescent outer border, gold stippled inner border, gold stencilled designs, two jewels decorated as opals.

PLATE 118, MOLD 57. Bowl, 10″d, gold decorated border mold flowers, floral center framed with gold stencilled design. (This mold also has been seen unmarked.)

The Collector's Encyclopedia of
R.S. Prussia
and other
R.S. and E.S. Porcelain
Price Guide

Prices for the R.S. Prussia and other R.S. and E.S. marked porcelain featured in this book show a **range** of prices for each item. The nature of today's market for Schlegelmilch porcelain makes it possible to establish such a "working" price range more easily than would have been the case a few years earlier. Today R.S. Prussia pieces are rarely "sleepers," and the other R.S. and E.S. marked pieces are recognized and valued by knowledgeable dealers and collectors.

The prices quoted in this guide are for pieces in mint condition. One must be aware that many factors enter into the price of an item that is asked or paid by dealers or collectors. The overall condition, the decoration, the type of finish, the type of mold, the specific object, the size, the scarcity, and the individual collector's need and desire for certain items--all play an important part in determining the ultimate price of a piece of Schlegelmilch porcelain.

The price range presented for the items in this guide was based on current prices asked or received by dealers, collectors, and auctioneers **specializing** in "Prussia." Only from such sources can realistic guidelines be obtained. As is true for all price guides, this one is to be used only as a **guide**. On occasion, some pieces may be offered or purchased well outside either end of the ranges quoted here. But every effort has been made to present figures which will enable the individual buyer, collector, dealer, or appraiser to place a value as accurately as possible on R.S. Prussia and other R.S. and E.S. marked porcelain.

The current values in this book should be used only as a guide. They are not intended to set prices, which vary from one section of the country to another. Auction prices as well as dealer prices vary greatly and are affected by condition as well as demand. Neither the Author nor the Publisher assumes responsibility for any losses that might be incurred as a result of consulting this guide.

COLLECTOR BOOKS
P.O. Box 3009
Paducah, KY 42001

Plate 35	$ 500.00- 700.00	Plate 100	$1,500.00-2,000.00	Plate 165	$ 200.00- 275.00
Plate 36	$ 450.00- 600.00	Plate 101	$1,500.00-2,000.00	Plate 166	$1,600.00-1,800.00
Plate 37	$ 400.00- 500.00	Plate 102	$ 300.00- 350.00	Plate 167	$1,200.00-1,400.00
Plate 38	$ 275.00- 350.00	Plate 103	$1,800.00-2,100.00	Plate 168	$ 600.00- 800.00
Plate 39	$ 275.00- 350.00	Plate 104	$1,400.00-1,600.00	Plate 169	$ 200.00- 275.00
Plate 40	$ 250.00- 300.00	Plate 105	$1,400.00-1,600.00	Plate 170	$ 250.00- 325.00
Plate 41	$ 300.00- 400.00	Plate 106	$ 700.00-1,000.00	Plate 171	$ 700.00- 900.00
Plate 42	$1,000.00-1,200.00	Plate 107	$ 300.00- 400.00	Plate 172	$1,000.00-1,200.00
Plate 43	$1,300.00-1,500.00	Plate 108	$ 300.00- 400.00	Plate 173	$1,000.00-1,200.00
Plate 44	$ 250.00- 350.00	Plate 109	$ 150.00- 200.00	Plate 174	$ 900.00-1,100.00
Plate 45	$ 750.00- 950.00	Plate 110	$ 225.00- 275.00	Plate 175	$ 150.00- 200.00
Plate 46	$1,300.00-1,600.00	Plate 111	$ 175.00- 250.00	Plate 176	$ 450.00- 600.00
Plate 47	$ 900.00-1,200.00	Plate 112	$ 175.00- 250.00	Plate 177	$ 150.00- 200.00
Plate 48	$ 400.00- 600.00	Plate 113	$ 275.00- 325.00	Plate 178	$ 250.00- 300.00
Plate 49	$ 175.00- 225.00	Plate 114	$ 275.00- 325.00	Plate 179	$ 250.00- 300.00
Plate 50	$ 275.00- 350.00	Plate 115	$ 175.00- 225.00	Plate 180	$ 400.00- 500.00
Plate 51	$1,500.00-2,000.00	Plate 116	$ 400.00- 600.00	Plate 181	$ 150.00- 200.00
Plate 52	$ 800.00-1,000.00	Plate 117	$ 200.00- 250.00	Plate 182	$ 250.00- 300.00
Plate 53	$ 275.00- 350.00	Plate 118	$ 300.00- 375.00	Plate 183	$ 75.00- 95.00
Plate 54	$ 250.00- 325.00	Plate 119	$ 75.00- 100.00	Plate 184	$2,200.00-2,500.00
Plate 55	$ 800.00-1,000.00	Plate 120	$ 90.00- 125.00	Plate 185	$ 275.00- 325.00
Plate 56	$1,100.00-1,300.00	Plate 121	$1,200.00-1,500.00	Plate 186	$2,200.00-2,500.00
Plate 57	$ 800.00-1,000.00	Plate 122	$ 500.00- 700.00	Plate 187	$ 200.00- 275.00
Plate 58	$1,600.00-1,800.00	Plate 123	$ 300.00- 400.00	Plate 188	$ 200.00- 275.00
Plate 59	$ 275.00- 325.00	Plate 124	$ 250.00- 300.00	Plate 189	$ 150.00- 200.00
Plate 60	$ 250.00- 300.00	Plate 125	$ 300.00- 400.00	Plate 190	$ 150.00- 200.00
Plate 61	$ 800.00-1,000.00	Plate 126	$ 300.00- 400.00	Plate 191	$ 250.00- 300.00
Plate 62	$ 225.00- 275.00	Plate 127	$ 450.00- 550.00	Plate 192	$ 175.00- 225.00
Plate 63	$ 75.00- 125.00	Plate 128	$ 300.00- 350.00	Plate 193	$1,200.00-1,400.00
Plate 64	$ 275.00- 325.00	Plate 129	$ 300.00- 350.00	Plate 194 . . (Set)	$1,600.00-1,800.00
Plate 65	$ 350.00- 450.00	Plate 130	$1,800.00-2,200.00	Plate 195	$ 150.00- 200.00
Plate 66	$ 350.00- 450.00	Plate 131	$ 400.00- 500.00	Plate 196	$ 150.00- 200.00
Plate 67	$ 300.00- 375.00	Plate 132	$ 225.00- 275.00	Plate 197	$ 275.00- 350.00
Plate 68	$1,500.00-2,000.00	Plate 133	$ 350.00- 450.00	Plate 198	$ 75.00- 100.00
Plate 69	$1,500.00-2,000.00	Plate 134	$ 200.00- 275.00	Plate 199 . (Each)	$ 50.00- 75.00
Plate 70	$ 450.00- 550.00	Plate 135	$ 175.00- 225.00	Plate 200	$ 275.00- 325.00
Plate 71	$ 250.00- 300.00	Plate 136	$1,500.00-2,000.00	Plate 201	$ 200.00- 300.00
Plate 72	$ 225.00- 275.00	Plate 137	$ 400.00- 500.00	Plate 202	$ 200.00- 300.00
Plate 73	$ 400.00- 500.00	Plate 138	$1,500.00-2,000.00	Plate 203	$ 200.00- 300.00
Plate 74	$ 400.00- 500.00	Plate 139	$ 300.00- 400.00	Plate 204	$ 200.00- 300.00
Plate 75	$ 275.00- 325.00	Plate 140	$ 300.00- 400.00	Plate 205	$ 250.00- 300.00
Plate 76	$ 400.00- 475.00	Plate 141	$ 300.00- 400.00	Plate 206	$ 250.00- 300.00
Plate 77	$ 225.00- 375.00	Plate 142	$ 300.00- 400.00	Plate 207	$ 275.00- 325.00
Plate 78	$1,000.00-1,200.00	Plate 143	$ 600.00- 700.00	Plate 208	$ 175.00- 225.00
Plate 79	$ 225.00- 300.00	Plate 144	$ 325.00- 400.00	Plate 209	$ 250.00- 300.00
Plate 80	$ 200.00- 250.00	Plate 145	$ 600.00- 800.00	Plate 210	$ 250.00- 300.00
Plate 81	$ 250.00- 300.00	Plate 146	$1,000.00-1,200.00	Plate 211	$ 150.00- 200.00
Plate 82	$ 300.00- 350.00	Plate 147	$ 275.00- 325.00	Plate 212	$ 175.00- 225.00
Plate 83	$1,500.00-2,000.00	Plate 148	$ 275.00- 325.00	Plate 213	$ 175.00- 225.00
Plate 84	$1,500.00-2,000.00	Plate 149	$ 500.00- 600.00	Plate 214	$ 275.00- 325.00
Plate 85	$1,500.00-1,800.00	Plate 150	$ 225.00- 275.00	Plate 215	$ 100.00- 150.00
Plate 86	$ 275.00- 325.00	Plate 151	$ 900.00-1,000.00	Plate 216	$ 350.00- 450.00
Plate 87	$ 225.00- 275.00	Plate 152	$1,600.00-1,800.00	Plate 217	$ 600.00- 800.00
Plate 88	$ 250.00- 300.00	Plate 153	$ 400.00- 600.00	Plate 218	$ 300.00- 400.00
Plate 89	$ 200.00- 250.00	Plate 154	$ 300.00- 400.00	Plate 219 . . (Set)	$ 800.00-1,000.00
Plate 90	$ 175.00- 225.00	Plate 155	$2,000.00-2,400.00	Plate 220	$ 275.00- 325.00
Plate 91	$ 175.00- 225.00	Plate 156	$ 300.00- 375.00	Plate 221	$ 300.00- 375.00
Plate 92	$ 175.00- 225.00	Plate 157	$ 300.00- 375.00	Plate 222	$ 275.00- 325.00
Plate 93	$ 400.00- 500.00	Plate 158	$ 500.00- 700.00	Plate 223	$ 250.00- 300.00
Plate 94	$2,000.00-2,400.00	Plate 159	$ 300.00- 400.00	Plate 224	$1,200.00-1,400.00
Plate 95 . . (Each)	$ 125.00- 175.00	Plate 160	$ 225.00- 275.00	Plate 225	$ 600.00- 800.00
Plate 96	$ 325.00- 400.00	Plate 161	$ 225.00- 275.00	Plate 226	$1,200.00-1,400.00
Plate 97	$ 300.00- 400.00	Plate 162 . (Each)	$ 75.00- 100.00	Plate 227	$ 100.00- 150.00
Plate 98	$ 500.00- 700.00	Plate 163	$ 150.00- 200.00	Plate 228	$ 175.00- 225.00
Plate 99	$1,200.00-1,500.00	Plate 164	$ 150.00- 200.00	Plate 229	$ 200.00- 250.00

Plate	Price	Plate	Price	Plate	Price
Plate 230	$ 225.00- 275.00	Plate 295	$ 400.00- 600.00	Plate 360	$ 900.00-1,100.00
Plate 231	$ 275.00- 325.00	Plate 296	$ 250.00- 300.00	Plate 361	$ 300.00- 350.00
Plate 232	$1,000.00-1,200.00	Plate 297	$ 150.00- 200.00	Plate 362	$ 300.00- 350.00
Plate 233	$ 800.00-1,000.00	Plate 298	$ 90.00- 125.00	Plate 363	$ 200.00- 225.00
Plate 234	$ 90.00- 125.00	Plate 299	$ 125.00- 150.00	Plate 364	$ 150.00- 175.00
Plate 235	$ 500.00- 700.00	Plate 300	$ 125.00- 150.00	Plate 365	$ 500.00- 600.00
Plate 236	$ 175.00- 225.00	Plate 301	$ 800.00-1,000.00	Plate 366	$ 150.00- 175.00
Plate 237	$ 200.00- 250.00	Plate 302	$ 125.00- 175.00	Plate 367	$ 150.00- 175.00
Plate 238	$ 100.00- 150.00	Plate 303	$ 225.00- 275.00	Plate 368	$1,200.00-1,400.00
Plate 239	$ 500.00- 600.00	Plate 304	$1,000.00-1,200.00	Plate 369	$ 300.00- 400.00
Plate 240	$ 300.00- 375.00	Plate 305	$ 600.00- 800.00	Plate 370	$ 225.00- 300.00
Plate 241	$ 300.00- 375.00	Plate 306	$ 300.00- 400.00	Plate 371	$ 700.00- 900.00
Plate 242	$ 300.00- 350.00	Plate 307	$ 225.00- 275.00	Plate 372	$ 225.00- 275.00
Plate 243	$ 450.00- 550.00	Plate 308	$ 175.00- 200.00	Plate 373	$5,000.00-6,000.00
Plate 244	$ 175.00- 225.00	Plate 309	$ 400.00- 500.00	Plate 374	$ 400.00- 500.00
Plate 245	$ 300.00- 350.00	Plate 310	$ 175.00- 225.00	Plate 375	$ 150.00- 200.00
Plate 246	$ 250.00- 300.00	Plate 311	$ 300.00- 400.00	Plate 376	$ 150.00- 175.00
Plate 247	$ 225.00- 275.00	Plate 312	$ 225.00- 275.00	Plate 377	$ 125.00- 150.00
Plate 248	$ 325.00- 375.00	Plate 313	$1,000.00-1,200.00	Plate 378	$1,000.00-1,200.00
Plate 249	$ 325.00- 400.00	Plate 314	$ 400.00- 500.00	Plate 379	$ 800.00-1,000.00
Plate 250	$ 225.00- 300.00	Plate 315	$ 250.00- 300.00	Plate 380	$ 200.00- 250.00
Plate 251	$ 300.00- 350.00	Plate 316	$ 300.00- 400.00	Plate 381	$ 125.00- 150.00
Plate 252	$ 375.00- 425.00	Plate 317	$ 90.00- 110.00	Plate 382	$ 600.00- 700.00
Plate 253	$2,000.00-2,400.00	Plate 318	$ 75.00- 100.00	Plate 383	$ 600.00- 800.00
Plate 254	$ 250.00- 300.00	Plate 319	$ 325.00- 375.00	Plate 384	Reverse of Plate 383
Plate 255	$ 225.00- 300.00	Plate 320	$ 350.00- 400.00	Plate 385	$ 200.00- 250.00
Plate 256	$ 75.00- 100.00	Plate 321	$ 325.00- 375.00	Plate 386	$ 400.00- 500.00
Plate 257	$ 90.00- 125.00	Plate 322	$ 400.00- 500.00	Plate 387	$ 300.00- 350.00
Plate 258	$1,800.00-2,000.00	Plate 323	$ 350.00- 400.00	Plate 388	$ 500.00- 700.00
Plate 259	$1,800.00-2,000.00	Plate 324	$ 150.00- 175.00	Plate 389	$1,500.00-1,800.00
Plate 260	$1,800.00-2,000.00	Plate 325	$1,400.00-1,600.00	Plate 390	$ 500.00- 700.00
Plate 261	$1,800.00-2,000.00	Plate 326	$ 175.00- 225.00	Plate 391	$1,400.00-1,600.00
Plate 262	$ 200.00- 250.00	Plate 327	$ 275.00- 325.00	Plate 392	$1,200.00-1,400.00
Plate 263	$ 175.00- 225.00	Plate 328	$ 300.00- 350.00	Plate 393	$ 225.00- 275.00
Plate 264	$ 150.00- 200.00	Plate 329	$ 350.00- 400.00	Plate 394	$ 250.00- 300.00
Plate 265	$ 175.00- 225.00	Plate 330	$1,200.00-1,500.00	Plate 395	$ 250.00- 300.00
Plate 266	$ 175.00- 225.00	Plate 331 . (Each)	$ 100.00- 125.00	Plate 396	$ 400.00- 500.00
Plate 267	$ 175.00- 225.00	Plate 332	$ 225.00- 275.00	Plate 397	$ 500.00- 700.00
Plate 268	$ 175.00- 225.00	Plate 333	$ 600.00- 800.00	Plate 398	$ 100.00- 150.00
Plate 269	$ 275.00- 325.00	Plate 334	$ 800.00-1,000.00	Plate 399	$ 400.00- 600.00
Plate 270	$1,000.00-1,200.00	Plate 335	$ 800.00-1,000.00	Plate 400	$1,400.00-1,600.00
Plate 271	$ 150.00- 200.00	Plate 336	$1,200.00-1,400.00	Plate 401	$ 500.00- 600.00
Plate 272	$ 150.00- 200.00	Plate 337	$ 900.00-1,100.00	Plate 402	$ 175.00- 225.00
Plate 273	$ 150.00- 200.00	Plate 338	$ 150.00- 200.00	Plate 403	$ 175.00- 225.00
Plate 274	$ 90.00- 125.00	Plate 339	$ 200.00- 250.00	Plate 404	$1,000.00-1,200.00
Plate 275	$ 150.00- 200.00	Plate 340	$ 350.00- 450.00	Plate 405	$1,400.00-1,600.00
Plate 276	$ 450.00- 600.00	Plate 341	$ 900.00-1,100.00	Plate 406	$ 600.00- 800.00
Plate 277	$ 200.00- 250.00	Plate 342	$ 900.00-1,100.00	Plate 407	$ 300.00- 400.00
Plate 278	$1,000.00-1,200.00	Plate 343	$ 900.00-1,100.00	Plate 408	$ 400.00- 500.00
Plate 279	$ 200.00- 250.00	Plate 344	$ 900.00-1,100.00	Plate 409	$ 600.00- 800.00
Plate 280	$ 250.00- 300.00	Plate 345	$1,200.00-1,400.00	Plate 410	$3,500.00-4,000.00
Plate 281	$ 125.00- 150.00	Plate 346	$ 700.00- 900.00	Plate 411	$ 700.00- 900.00
Plate 282	$1,600.00-1,800.00	Plate 347	$ 800.00-1,000.00	Plate 412	$ 225.00- 300.00
Plate 283	$ 125.00- 150.00	Plate 348 . . (Set)	$1,700.00-2,000.00	Plate 413	$ 600.00- 800.00
Plate 284	$ 300.00- 375.00	Plate 349	$ 250.00- 300.00	Plate 414	$1,000.00-1,200.00
Plate 285	$1,200.00-1,400.00	Plate 350 . . (Set)	$1,400.00-1,600.00	Plate 415	$1,400.00-1,600.00
Plate 286	$ 225.00- 300.00	Plate 351	$ 200.00- 250.00	Plate 416	$1,000.00-1,200.00
Plate 287	$ 200.00- 250.00	Plate 352	$ 200.00- 250.00	Plate 417	$1,800.00-2,000.00
Plate 288	$1,000.00-1,200.00	Plate 353	$ 300.00- 350.00	Plate 418	$ 150.00- 175.00
Plate 289	$ 100.00- 125.00	Plate 354	$1,000.00-1,200.00	Plate 419	$ 100.00- 125.00
Plate 290	$ 125.00- 150.00	Plate 355	$1,000.00-1,200.00	Plate 420	$ 600.00- 800.00
Plate 291	$ 150.00- 175.00	Plate 356	$1,000.00-1,200.00	Plate 421	$ 500.00- 600.00
Plate 292	$ 200.00- 275.00	Plate 357	$1,000.00-1,200.00	Plate 422	$ 125.00- 150.00
Plate 293	$1,000.00-1,200.00	Plate 358	$ 300.00- 400.00	Plate 423	$ 275.00- 325.00
Plate 294	$1,000.00-1,200.00	Plate 359	$ 500.00- 600.00	Plate 424	$ 250.00- 300.00

Plate 425	$ 300.00- 400.00	Plate 476	$ 250.00- 300.00	Plate 526	$ 35.00- 45.00
Plate 426	$ 300.00- 400.00	Plate 477	$ 300.00- 400.00	Plate 527	$ 25.00- 35.00
Plate 427	$ 275.00- 325.00	Plate 478	$1,600.00-1,800.00	Plate 528	$ 25.00- 35.00
Plate 428	$ 250.00- 300.00	Plate 479	$ 450.00- 600.00	Plate 529	$ 30.00- 40.00
Plate 429	$ 200.00- 275.00	Plate 480	$1,200.00-1,400.00	Plate 530	$ 35.00- 45.00
Plate 430	$ 275.00- 325.00	Plate 481	$1,000.00-1,200.00	Plate 531	$ 50.00- 60.00
Plate 431	$ 125.00- 175.00	Plate 482	Reverse side of	Plate 532	$ 25.00- 35.00
Plate 432	$ 175.00- 225.00		Plate 481	Plate 533	$ 25.00- 35.00
Plate 433	$ 175.00- 225.00	Plate 483	$ 400.00- 600.00	Plate 534	$ 25.00- 35.00
Plate 434	$ 200.00- 300.00	Plate 484	$ 400.00- 600.00	Plate 535	$ 175.00- 225.00
Plate 435	$ 150.00- 200.00	Plate 485	$ 400.00- 600.00	Plate 536	$ 300.00- 400.00
Plate 436	$ 225.00- 300.00	Plate 486	$ 400.00- 600.00	Plate 537	$ 275.00- 375.00
Plate 437	$ 300.00- 400.00	Plate 487	$ 250.00- 300.00	Plate 538	$ 400.00- 500.00
Plate 438	$ 400.00- 500.00	Plate 488	$ 125.00- 175.00	Plate 539	$ 150.00- 200.00
Plate 439	$ 325.00- 400.00	Plate 489	$ 35.00- 50.00	Plate 540	$ 300.00- 400.00
Plate 440	$ 350.00- 450.00	Plate 490	$ 125.00- 175.00	Plate 541	$ 175.00- 225.00
Plate 441	$ 450.00- 600.00	Plate 491	$ 150.00- 200.00	Plate 542	$ 100.00- 150.00
Plate 442	$ 750.00- 900.00	Plate 492	$ 40.00- 60.00	Plate 543	$ 90.00- 125.00
Plate 443	$ 500.00- 700.00	Plate 493	$ 45.00- 65.00	Plate 544	$ 90.00- 125.00
Plate 444	$1,800.00-2,000.00	Plate 494	$ 150.00- 200.00	Plate 545	$ 100.00- 150.00
Plate 445	$1,000.00-1,200.00	Plate 495	$ 800.00-1,000.00	Plate 546	$ 60.00- 80.00
Plate 446	$1,800.00-2,000.00	Plate 496	$ 300.00- 400.00	Plate 547	$ 40.00- 50.00
Plate 447	$1,800.00-2,000.00	Plate 497	$ 400.00- 600.00	Plate 548	$ 125.00- 175.00
Plate 448	$1,800.00-2,000.00	Plate 498	$ 500.00- 600.00	Plate 549	$ 25.00- 40.00
Plate 449	$1,800.00-2,000.00	Plate 499	$ 275.00- 325.00	Plate 550	$ 175.00- 225.00
Plate 450	$ 600.00- 800.00	Plate 500	$ 300.00- 400.00	Plate 551	$ 30.00- 40.00
Plate 451	$ 500.00- 700.00	Plate 501	$ 125.00- 175.00	Plate 552	$ 125.00- 175.00
Plate 452	$1,800.00-2,000.00	Plate 502	$ 225.00- 275.00	Plate 553	$ 90.00- 125.00
Plate 453	$ 350.00- 500.00	Plate 503	$ 225.00- 300.00	Plate 554	$ 60.00- 75.00
Plate 454	$1,000.00-1,200.00	Plate 504	$ 175.00- 225.00	Plate 555	$ 50.00- 75.00
Plate 455	$ 700.00-1,000.00	Plate 505	$ 90.00- 125.00	Plate 556	$ 25.00- 35.00
Plate 456	$ 600.00- 800.00	Plate 506	$ 90.00- 125.00	Plate 557	$ 30.00- 40.00
Plate 457	$ 300.00- 350.00	Plate 507	$ 90.00- 125.00	Plate 558	$ 40.00- 50.00
Plate 458	$ 275.00- 325.00	Plate 508	$ 90.00- 125.00	Plate 559	$ 45.00- 65.00
Plate 459	$ 300.00- 350.00	Plate 509	$ 100.00- 140.00	Plate 560	$ 60.00- 80.00
Plate 460	$ 225.00- 275.00	Plate 510	$ 90.00- 125.00	Plate 561	$ 45.00- 55.00
Plate 461	$ 275.00- 325.00	Plate 511	$ 300.00- 400.00	Plate 562	$ 20.00- 30.00
Plate 462	$ 350.00- 500.00	Plate 512	$ 75.00- 100.00	Plate 563	$ 25.00- 35.00
Plate 463	$ 225.00- 275.00	Plate 513	$ 90.00- 125.00	Plate 564	$ 90.00- 125.00
Plate 464	$ 275.00- 325.00	Plate 514	$ 75.00- 100.00	Plate 565	Price not available
Plate 465 . (Each)	$ 90.00- 125.00	Plate 515	$ 90.00- 125.00	Plate 566	$ 300.00- 400.00
Plate 466	$ 500.00- 700.00	Plate 516	$ 100.00- 125.00	Plate 567	$ 125.00- 175.00
Plate 467	$ 125.00- 200.00	Plate 517	$ 60.00- 80.00	Plate 568	$ 90.00- 135.00
Plate 468	$1,200.00-1,400.00	Plate 518	$ 60.00- 80.00	Plate 569	$ 75.00- 100.00
Plate 469	$ 175.00- 225.00	Plate 519	$ 175.00- 225.00	Plate 570	$ 175.00- 250.00
Plate 470	$ 600.00- 800.00	Plate 520	$ 150.00- 200.00	Plate 571	$ 250.00- 300.00
Plate 471	$ 90.00- 125.00	Plate 521	$ 50.00- 70.00	Plate 572	$ 100.00- 150.00
Plate 472	$ 500.00- 700.00	Plate 522	$ 75.00- 100.00	Plate 573	$ 45.00- 55.00
Plate 473	$ 225.00- 300.00	Plate 523	$ 25.00- 35.00	Plate 574	$ 500.00- 700.00
Plate 474	$ 175.00- 200.00	Plate 524	$ 30.00- 40.00	Plate 575	$ 300.00- 400.00
Plate 475	$ 95.00- 125.00	Plate 525	$ 45.00- 55.00	Plate 576 . (Pair)	$ 700.00- 800.00

Unusual Body Shapes (Plates 119 to 159)

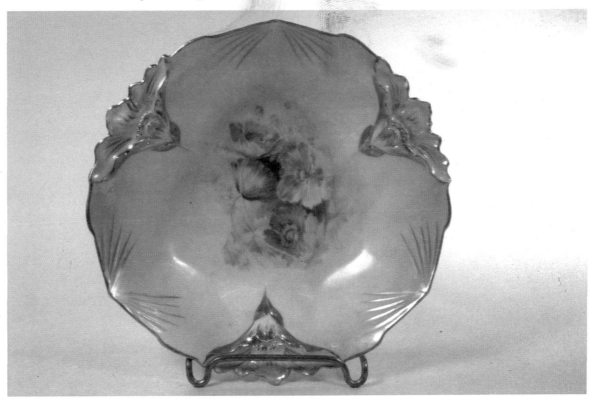

PLATE 119, MOLD 76. Bowl, 5½"d, blown out three part mold.

PLATE 120, MOLD 77. Bowl, 5½"d, blown out three part mold, 3 undecorated jewels.

PLATE 121, MOLD 78. Tray, 12″l, 7½″w, 6 double dome sections, Autumn portrait.

PLATE 122, MOLD 78. Berry Set, Master Bowl, 10½″d, 5 double dome sections; individual bowls (4), 5½″d, 3 double dome sections.

PLATE 123, MOLD 78. Bowl, 10½″d, 5 double dome sections.

PLATE 124, MOLD 78. Plate, 7½″d, 5 double dome sections, handpainted, artist signed "Happ." in center. RSP Mark 4 and RSG Mark 9.

PLATE 125, MOLD 79. Bowl, 10½″d, 5 single dome shapes.

PLATE 126, MOLD 80. Bowl, 10½″d, 5 reverse dome shapes.

PLATE 127, MOLD 81. Bowl, 8″d, 3″h, 3 footed, 5 single dome sections with 3 jewels each decorated as opals, red iridescent finish on domes.

PLATE 128, MOLD 82. Cake Plate, 11″d, 6 dome sections with 5 jewels each, undecorated.

PLATE 129, MOLD 82. Bowl, 9″d.

PLATE 130, MOLD 82. Bowl, 10½″d, Melon Eaters.

PLATE 131, MOLD 83. Bowl, 11"d, 6 blown out sections.

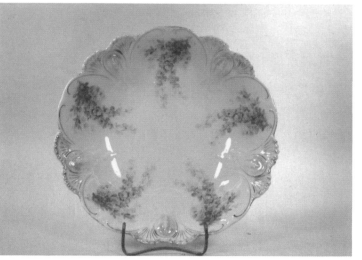

132, MOLD 84. Bowl, 10½"d, 5 rounded blown out sections, pearl finish with pearl lustre on embossed leaf designs between blown out sections.

PLATE 133, MOLD 85. Bowl, 10"d, 5 blown out dome sections, ornate floral and leaf border, 5 jewels.

PLATE 134, MOLD 86. Bowl, 10½"d, 6 shallow squared dome sections, very dark bkgrd, Dresden floral decor. Unmarked.

PLATE 135, MOLD 86. Bowl, 10½"d. Unmarked.

PLATE 136, MOLD 87. Bowl, 10″d, 6 blown out dome sections, Lebrun portrait, green iridescent Tiffany finish. Unmarked.

PLATE 137, MOLD 87. Bowl, 10″d. Unmarked.

PLATE 138, MOLD 87. Bowl, 10″d, Lebrun portrait, bronze iridescent Tiffany finish.

PLATE 139, MOLD 88. Bowl, 10½″d, 5 expanded dome sections, Roses.

PLATE 140, MOLD 88. Bowl, 10½″d, Water Lilies.

PLATE 141, MOLD 89. Bowl, 11″d, 5 expanded dome sections, Roses, gold stencilled designs.

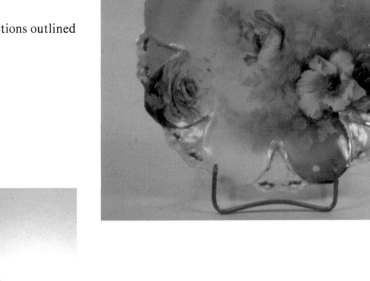

PLATE 142, MOLD 90. Plate, 8½″d, 8 dome sections outlined in mold. Poppies.

PLATE 143, MOLD 90. Berry Set, Master Bowl, 8½″d, individual bowls (6), 6″d with 5 dome sections, Poppies.

PLATE 144, MOLD 90. Bowl, 10½″d, RSP Mark 5.

PLATE 145, MOLD 90. Plate, 8½"d, Mill scene.

PLATE 146, MOLD 90. Bowl, 10"d, Mill scene.

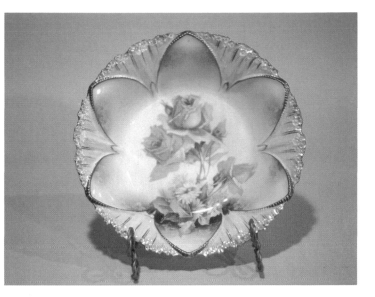

PLATE 147, MOLD 91. Bowl, 10½″d, 6 single dome shapes outlined by beaded border in mold, Roses.

PLATE 148, MOLD 91. Bowl, 10″d, Roses and Daisies.

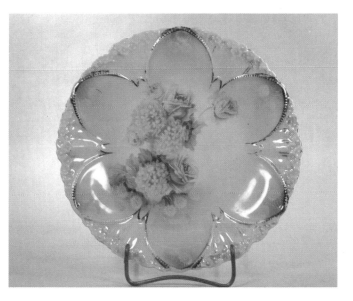

PLATE 149, MOLD 91. Berry Set, Master Bowl, 10″d, individual bowls (6), 5½″d with 5 dome sections, Roses.

PLATE 150, MOLD 91. Plate, 9″d, Roses and Snowballs.

PLATE 151, MOLD 92. Plate, 8″d, 8 dome sections, high glaze finish, Turkey and evergreens, gold stencilled designs.

PLATE 152, MOLD 92. Plate, 8½″d, Snowbird winter scene, gold stencilled designs.

PLATE 153, MOLD 93. Plate, 6″d, 8 dome sections, Castle scene.

PLATE 154, MOLD 94. Bowl, 10½″d, 7 dome sections, Roses.

PLATE 155, MOLD 95. Bowl, 10½″d, 6 star points in mold, double portrait decor of Autumn (top) and Winter (bottom). "Germany" in gold mark in addition to RSP mark.

PLATE 156, MOLD 96. Bowl, 11″d, 6 star points, Roses and Snowballs.

PLATE 157, MOLD 96. Bowl, 11″d, Roses and Snowballs.

PLATE 158, MOLD 97. Berry Set, Master Bowl, 10½″d, 10 star points, individual bowls, 5½″d (6), 5 star points.

PLATE 159, MOLD 98. Bowl, 10″d, 12 star points, unmarked.

Border Molds (Pointed — Plates 160 to 171)

PLATE 160, MOLD 151. Cake Plate, 12″d.

PLATE 161, MOLD 151. Cake Plate, 10″d.

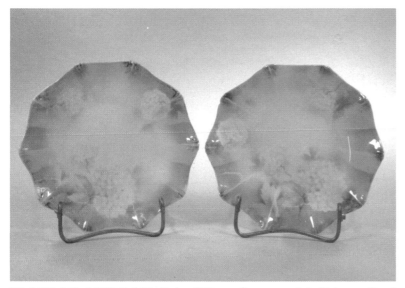

PLATE 162, MOLD 151. Pair of Plates from set of 6, 6″d, pearlized lustre finish.

PLATE 163, MOLD 152. Footed Bowl, 6½″d, 2½″, pearl finish.

PLATE 164, MOLD 153. Footed Bowl, 7½″d, 2½″h.

PLATE 165, MOLD 154. Bowl, 9½″d, single and double notched indentations on border, faint dome shapes inside mold.

PLATE 166, MOLD 155. Bowl, 11"d, pointed and notched border, Peafowl decor, high glaze on outer border.

PLATE 167, MOLD 155. Bowl, 10½"d, Sheepherder I decor, high glaze on outer border.

PLATE 168, MOLD 155. Berry Set, Master Bowl, 11"d, individual bowls (6), 5½"d, Hanging Basket decor, high glaze on outer border.

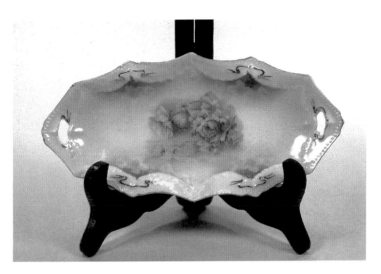

PLATE 169, MOLD 155. Relish, 8"l, 4"w, Reflecting poppies and daisies.

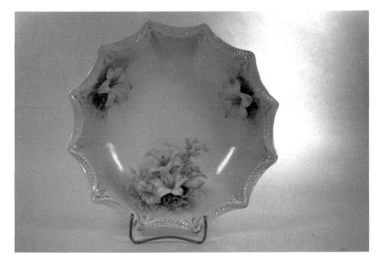

PLATE 170, MOLD 156. Bowl, 11"d, border composed of equal sized points, Lily of the Valley decor, pearl lustre on inner beaded border.

PLATE 171, MOLD 157. Bowl, 11"d, points on border alternate with floral clusters, Swallow decor.

Border Molds (Rounded Scallops — Plates 172 to 177)

PLATE 172, MOLD 181. Bowl, 10″d, Castle scene.

PLATE 173, MOLD 181. Bowl, 10″d, Mill scene.

PLATE 174, MOLD 182. Cake Plate, 9″d, Victorian Vignette decor.

PLATE 175, MOLD 182. Relish, 9½″l, 4½″w, satin finish, Dogwood blossoms, gold stencilled designs.

PLATE 176, MOLD 182. Berry Set, Master Bowl, 9½″d, individual bowls (5), 5″d, satin finish, Dogwood blossoms, gold stencilled designs.

PLATE 177, MOLD 182. Receiving Card Tray, 6″l, 3″w, Dogwood blossoms, gold stencilled designs.

Border Molds (Semi-round Scallops — Plates 178 to 200)

PLATE 178, MOLD 201. Bowl, 10½″d, pearlized lustre on outer border.

PLATE 179, MOLD 201. Bowl, 10½″d, roses and daisies.

PLATE 180, MOLD 201. Bowl, 10½″d, satin finish.

PLATE 181, MOLD 202. Plate, 8½″d, pearl finish. Unmarked pieces and RSG marked pieces also have been seen in this mold.

PLATE 182, MOLD 202. Cake Plate, 11½″d, Pair of Swans.

PLATE 183, MOLD 202. Bowl, 5″d, Underplate, 6″d, pearlized lustre finish, unmarked.

PLATE 184, MOLD 202. Bowl, 11″d, Stag scene, satin finish.

PLATE 185, MOLD 203. Bowl, 10″d, blown out sections under semi-round scalloped border.

PLATE 186, MOLD 203. Bowl, 11″d, Stag scene, satin finish.

PLATE 187, MOLD 204. Bowl, 10″d, concave "V" shaped sections separate semi-round scallops, satin finish.

PLATE 188, MOLD 204. Bowl, 10″d.

PLATE 189, MOLD 205. Plate, 9″d, convex sections separate semi-round scallops, satin finish.

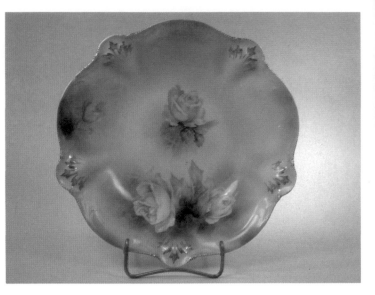

PLATE 190, MOLD 205. Bowl, 9½″d, satin finish.

PLATE 191, MOLD 206. Bowl, 9½″d, thickly beaded semi-round scalloped border, satin finish on border.

PLATE 192, MOLD 207. Celery, 12″l, 7″w, rounded convex shapes separate semi-round scallops.

PLATE 193, MOLD 207. Oval Bowl, 13″l, 9″w, Masted Ship decor, gold stencilled designs, high glaze finish.

PLATE 194, MOLD 207. Cake Service, Cake Plate, 11″d, individual plates (6), 6″d, Masted Ship decor, pearlized lustre finish.

PLATE 195, MOLD 208. Cake Plate, 10″d, Roses and Surreal Dogwood decor, pearlized lustre finish, RSP Mark 5.

PLATE 196, MOLD 208. Plate, 8½″d, matches Plate 195 in decor.

PLATE 197, MOLD 209. Cake Plate, 12″d, Surreal Dogwood decor, satin finish.

PLATE 198, Mold 210. Plate, 9½″d, small points separate semi-round scallops on border.

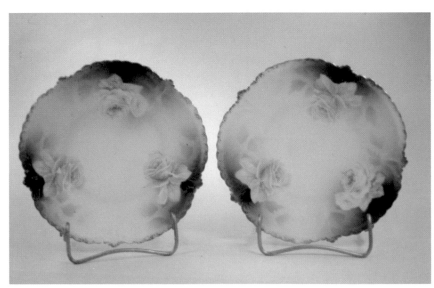

PLATE 199, MOLD 210. Pair of Plates from set of 6, 6½″d, unmarked.

PLATE 200, MOLD 211. Bowl, 10½″d, deeply fluted semi-round scallops on outer border.

Border Molds (Crimped Scallops — Plates 201 to 218)

PLATE 201, MOLD 251. Cake Plate, 12″d, satin finish.

PLATE 202, MOLD 251. Cake Plate, 12″d, pearl lustre finish, gold enamelling.

PLATE 203, MOLD 251. Cake Plate, 12″d, satin finish.

PLATE 204, MOLD 251. Cake Plate, 10″d, satin finish.

PLATE 205, MOLD 252. Bowl, 10½″d, satin finish. This mold also has been seen with an RSG mark.

PLATE 206 MOLD 252. Bowl, 10½″d, pearlized finish.

PLATE 207, MOLD 252. Celery, 14″l, 7″w, satin finish, gold stippling on flowers, inner gold stencilled border.

PLATE 208, MOLD 253. Celery, 12½″l, 6″w, concave sections separate crimped scalloped border.

PLATE 209, MOLD 254. Bowl, 10½"d, satin finish on border.

PLATE 210, MOLD 254. Bowl, 9"d, pearlized lustre border.

PLATE 211, MOLD 255. Relish, 9"l, 4"w, pearlized lustre finish, Surreal Dogwood Blossoms, gold enamelling.

PLATE 212, MOLD 256. Plate, 8"d, pearlized lustre finish, gold enamelling.

PLATE 213, MOLD 256. Cake Plate, 11½"d, pearlized lustre finish, Surreal Dogwood Blossoms, gold enamelling.

PLATE 214, MOLD 257. Bowl, 10½″d, satin finish inside border.

PLATE 215, MOLD 258. Plate, 9″d, deeply crimped scalloped border.

PLATE 216, MOLD 259. Bowl, 11"d, pearl button finish.

PLATE 217, MOLD 259. Berry Set, Master Bowl, 11"d, individual bowls (6), 5"d, pearl button finish.

PLATE 218, MOLD 259. Cake Plate, 10″d, pearl button finish. Unmarked.

Border Molds (Wavy Scallops — Plates 219 to 223)

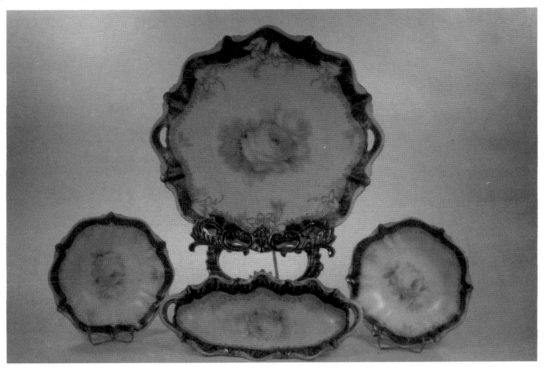

PLATE 219, MOLD 276. Dessert Service, Cake Plate, 9½"d, individual bowls (4), 5"d, Bonbon dish, 8"l, 4"w, satin finish, bronze iridescent Tiffany trim.

PLATE 220, Mold 276. Bowl, 10"d, pearlized lustre border.

PLATE 221, MOLD 276. Cake Plate, 11½"d, satin finish, gold stencilled designs.

PLATE 222, MOLD 277. Bowl, 10″d, pearlized lustre border, Calla Lily decor.

PLATE 223, MOLD 277. Bowl, 10½″d, pearlized lustre border.

Border Molds (Elongated Scallops — Plates 224 to 235)

PLATE 224, MOLD 300. Plate, 8½″d, Dice Throwers.

PLATE 225, MOLD 300. Plate, 8½″d, Castle scene.

PLATE 226, MOLD 300. Celery, 13½″l, 7″w, Melon Eaters.

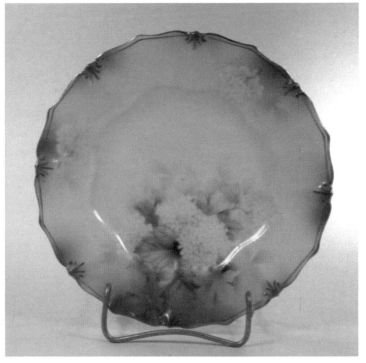

PLATE 227, MOLD 301. Plate, 8″d, recessed center, Snow-balls.

PLATE 228, MOLD 302. Cake Plate, 10″d, pearlized lustre finish, Surreal Dogwood Blossoms.

PLATE 229, MOLD 302. Plate, 10″d.

PLATE 230, MOLD 303. Bowl, 10½″d.

PLATE 231, MOLD 303. Bowl, 10½″d, Swan decor, satin finish, gold enamelling and gold stippling on flowers, unmarked.

PLATE 232, MOLD 304. Plate, 7½"d, beaded elongated border scallops, Turkey with Evergreens decor, pearlized lustre border.

PLATE 233, MOLD 304. Oval Bun Tray, 13"l, 8½"w, Swans through Evergreens scene, pearlized lustre finish.

PLATE 234, MOLD 305. Plate, 8″d, small concave sections separate elongated scallops on border, pearlized lustre on border.

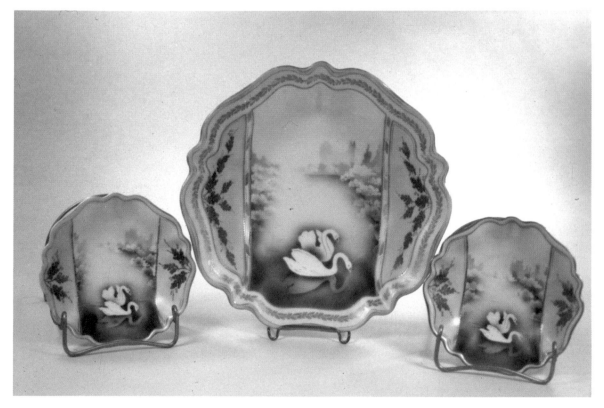

PLATE 235, MOLD 305. Berry Set, Master Bowl, 9″d, individual bowls (6), 5″d, Pair of Swans, satin and matte finish.

Border Molds (Irregular Scallops — Plates 236 to 261)

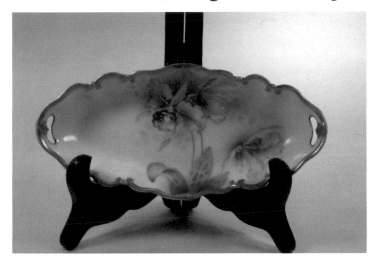

PLATE 236, MOLD 326. Relish, 8"l, 4"w.

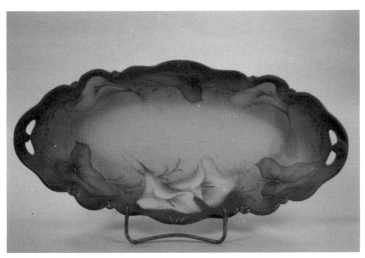

PLATE 237, MOLD 326. Celery, 12"l, 6"w, matte finish, Calla Lilies.

PLATE 238, MOLD 327. Pin Tray, 6"l, pearlized lustre, Lily.

PLATE 239, MOLD 327. Tray, 12"l, 9"w, Swans with Gazebo scene.

PLATE 240, MOLD 328. Bowl, 11″d, Cottage scene, unmarked.

PLATE 241, MOLD 328. Bowl, 11″d, Castle scene, unmarked.

PLATE 242, MOLD 329. Bowl, 10½"d, Roses and Snowballs.

PLATE 243, MOLD 329. Berry Set, Master Bowl, 10½"d, individual bowls (5), 5½"d, Roses and Snowballs. Note individual bowls are not a mold match to Master bowl.

PLATE 244, MOLD 330. Plate, 9″d, pearlized lustre finish, Floral and Berry decor.

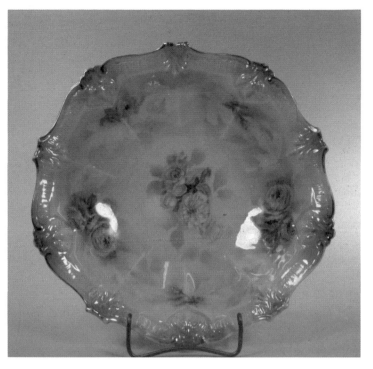

PLATE 245, MOLD 331. Bowl, 11"d, satin finish, Roses center.

PLATE 246, MOLD 332. Bowl, ll"d, pearlized lustre, Roses.

PLATE 247, MOLD 333. Cake Plate, 11½"d, Roses, gold stencilled inner border.

PLATE 248, MOLD 334. Bowl, ll"d, recessed center, Reflecting Poppies and Daisies.

PLATE 249, MOLD 335. Ambrosia Bowl, 8½"d, 4"h, Holly and white floral decor, gold enamelling.

PLATE 250, MOLD 336. Tray, 10½"l, 6½"w, Roses, gold enamelling.

PLATE 251, MOLD 337. Bowl, 11"d, satin finish on border.

PLATE 252, MOLD 338. Bowl, 11"d, gold border, satin and watered silk finish.

PLATE 253, MOLD 339. Bowl, 11″d, Récamier portrait, bronze iridescent Tiffany finish.

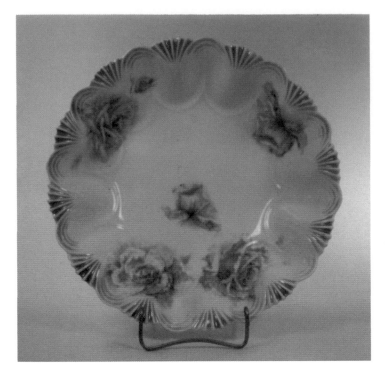

PLATE 254, MOLD 340. Bowl, 10½″d, pearlized lustre on border.

PLATE 255, MOLD 341. Cake Plate, 11″d, satin finish.

PLATE 256, MOLD 342. Plate, 6″d, Roses.

PLATE 257, MOLD 342. Plate, 7½″d, matte finish on border, Roses.

PLATE 258, MOLD 343. Plate, 9″d, Summer portrait, "keyhole" frame. Note this mold is also seen with the RSG Steeple Mark.

PLATE 259, MOLD 343. Plate, 9″d, Spring portrait.

PLATE 260, MOLD 343. Plate, 9″d, Autumn portrait.

PLATE 261, MOLD 343. Plate, 9″d, Winter portrait.

Border Molds (Scroll borders — Plates 262 to 269)

PLATE 262, MOLD 401. Bowl, 11″d, ornate scrolled border, high glaze finish, unmarked.

PLATE 263, MOLD 401. Bowl, 10½″d, turquoise tapestry finish on gold trim, unmarked.

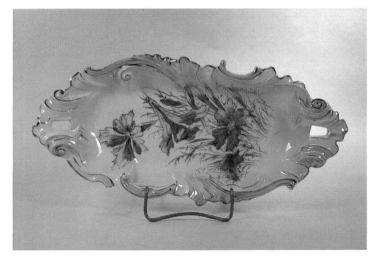

PLATE 264, MOLD 401. Celery, 14″l, pearl lustre finish on borders, unmarked.

PLATE 265, MOLD 401. Bowl, 10″d, floral decor, unmarked.

PLATE 266, MOLD 402. Bowl, 10″d, scroll and floral border, pearl lustre finish on border, unmarked.

PLATE 267, MOLD 402. Bowl, 10″d, Poppies, unmarked.

PLATE 268, MOLD 402. Bowl, 10″d, Poppies, unmarked.

PLATE 269, MOLD 403. Bowl, 10½″d, scroll and floral border, watered silk finish. This mold has also been seen unmarked.

Border Molds (Smooth borders — Plates 270 to 273)

PLATE 270, MOLD 426. Wall Plaque, Man in the Mountain scene, 8½"d.

PLATE 271, MOLD 427. Bread Tray, 11"l, 8"w, handpainted, RSP Mark 6 and Germany impressed.

PLATE 272, MOLD 428. Bread Tray, 11"l, 7"w.

PLATE 273, MOLD 429. Bread Tray, 12"l, 7"w, Dogwood Blossoms.

Vertical Objects (Smooth bases — Plates 274 to 294)

PLATE 274, MOLD 451. Covered Sugar, 4″h, 6″w, pearlized lustre finish, Lily decor. Unmarked pieces also have been seen in this mold.

PLATE 275, MOLD 451. Syrup Pitcher, 4″h, pearlized lustre finish, Surreal Dogwood Blossoms, gold enamelling.

PLATE 276, MOLD 451. Covered Butter Dish, 6″h, 8½″w with liner (not shown), Surreal Dogwood Blossoms, gold enamelling.

PLATE 277, MOLD 451. Creamer, 3½″h, Sugar, 3½″h, pearlized lustre finish, Surreal Dogwood Blossoms, gold enamelling.

PLATE 278, MOLD 452. Chocolate Pot, 10″h, satin finish, Swans.

PLATE 279, MOLD 452. Covered Sugar, 6″h, 6½″w, Creamer, 4″h. Cover of Sugar varies from mold (see Plate 278).

PLATE 280, MOLD 452. Sugar, 2½″h, Creamer, 2½″h, Roses.

PLATE 281, MOLD 453. Cup 2½″h, 3½″w, Floral decor.

PLATE 282. MOLD 454, Chocolate Set, Pot, 11″h, Cups, (6) 3″h satin finish.

PLATE 283, MOLD 454. Coffee Cup, 2½″h, pearl lustre finish.

PLATE 284, MOLD 455. Covered Sugar, 4½″h, Victorian figural "Lady Watering Flowers."

120

PLATE 285, MOLD 456. Covered Sugar, 5″h, 5″w, Creamer, 3″h, Winter portrait.

PLATE 286, MOLD 457. Cracker Jar, 6″h, 9″w, Roses, gold stippled border.

PLATE 287. MOLD 458, Cracker Jar, 6½″h, 9″w, square body mold with handles formed from mold.

PLATE 288. MOLD 459. Chocolate Set. Pot, 8″h, Cups (5) 3″h, Floral decor, gold stippled border and gold stencilled designs, ornate squared handles.

PLATE 289, MOLD 460. Cup, 3″h, gold tapestry work, question mark shaped handle.

PLATE 290, MOLD 461. Demi-Tasse Cup, 3″h, satin finish, gold stencilled inner border, spattered gold outer border.

PLATE 291, MOLD 462. Cup, 3½″h, stippled gold shield and Roses, rococo question mark handle.

PLATE 292, MOLD 462. Mustache Cup, 3½″h, gold scroll work, Roses.

PLATE 293, MOLD 463. Chocolate set (Sunflower Mold), Pot, 8″h, Cups, 3″h, double twisted handles. Also see Plate 374 in Vertical Objects and Plates 107 and 108 in Flat Objects.

PLATE 294, MOLD 464. Humidor, 6 sided, Roses and Snowballs.

PLATE 295, MOLD 501. Covered Sugar, 5"h, 6"w, Creamer 3"h, deeply crimped border, incised fan shapes, curved looped handles, iridescent Tiffany finish on mid section, unmarked.

PLATE 296, MOLD 501. Cracker Jar, 6½"h, 7"w, RSP Mark 15.

PLATE 297, MOLD 501. 3 Handled Toothpick Holder, 2"h, pearlized lustre finish, Surreal Dogwood Blossoms, gold enamelling.

PLATE 298, MOLD 501. Creamer, 3½"h, gold spattered border, unmarked.

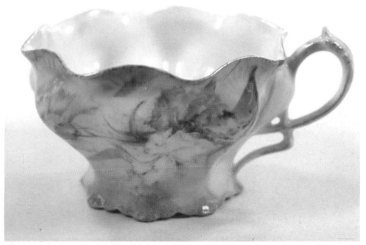

PLATE 299, MOLD 501. Cup, 2½"h, Carnations.

PLATE 300, MOLD 501. Cup, 2½"h, pearlized lustre finish, Surreal Dogwood Blossoms, gold enamelling.

PLATE 301, MOLD 502. Chocolate Set, Pot, 10"h, Cups, 3½"h, two part extended handle, Snowballs with enamelling, unmarked. (RSP marked examples have been seen in this mold, see Plate 439.)

PLATE 302, MOLD 502. Mustard Pot, 3½"h, Roses, unmarked.

PLATE 303, MOLD 502. Cracker Jar, 6"h, 5"d, handle variation, unmarked.

PLATE 304, MOLD 503. Chocolate Set, Pot, 10½"h, Cups, 3"h (4), flared top, pierced handle on Chocolate Pot but not on Cups.

PLATE 305, MOLD 504. Tea Set, Pot, 6″h, Sugar, 4″h, Creamer, 3½″h, "Bow Tie" finial and in relief at top of mold, handle is similar to Mold 466 (Plates 301 and 302), unmarked.

PLATE 306, MOLD 505. Covered Sugar, 4″h, Creamer, 3½″h, cameo portraits, unmarked.

PLATE 307, MOLD 505. Cracker Jar, 7½″h, 7″w, pearl lustre border, high glaze finish, RSP Mark 5.

PLATE 308, MOLD 506. Covered Sugar, 4″h, 6″w, crown finial, gold stencilled designs.

PLATE 309, MOLD 507. Chocolate Pot, 10½″h, Floral decor.

PLATE 310, MOLD 507. Mustard Pot with spoon, 3½″h.

PLATE 311, MOLD 507. Tea Pot, 6½″h, satin finish.

PLATE 312, MOLD 507. Cracker Jar, 4½″h, 6″w, Roses.

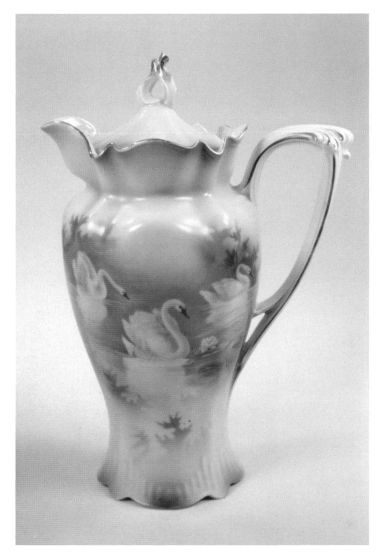

PLATE 313, MOLD 508. Chocolate Pot, 9½"h, Swans.

PLATE 314, Mold 509. Chocolate Pot, 11"h, pearlized lustre finish.

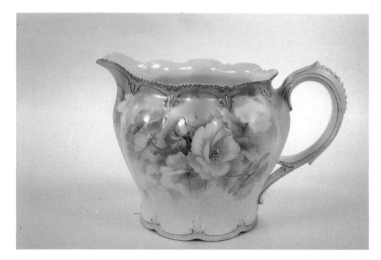

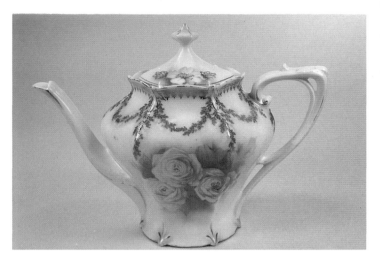

PLATE 315, MOLD 510. Cider Pitcher, 6½″ h, satin finish.

PLATE 316, MOLD 511. Tea Pot, 7″ h, 6 sided top, satin finish.

PLATE 317, MOLD 512. Covered Sugar, 5″ h, 6″ w, Floral decor.

PLATE 318, MOLD 513. Cup, 2″ h, Roses.

PLATE 319, MOLD 514. "Iris Variation" Mold, Pitcher, 10"h, unmarked. Also see Plates 88 to 93 in Flat Objects.

PLATE 320, MOLD 514. "Iris Variation" Mold. Chocolate Pot, 10"h, unmarked.

PLATE 321, MOLD 515. "Hidden Images" Mold, unmarked. Also see Plates 39 to 41 in Flat Objects for similar Molds.

PLATE 322, MOLD 516. Chocolate Pot, 9½"h, satin finish, Reflecting Water Lilies, unmarked.

PLATE 323, MOLD 517. Chocolate Pot, 10″h, raised floral designs as part of border, unmarked.

PLATE 324, MOLD 518. "Iris" Mold, Cup, 3½″h. Also see Plates 378 to 380 in Vertical Objects and Plates 83 to 87 in Flat Objects.

PLATE 325, MOLD 519. "Carnation" Mold, Covered Sugar, 5½″h, Creamer, 4″h, satin finish, Summer portrait. Also see Plates 341 to 351 in Vertical Objects and Plates 94 to 99 in Flat Objects.

PLATE 326, MOLD 520. Vase, 4½″h, embossed roses on handles.

PLATE 327, MOLD 521. Covered Sugar, 5½″h, Creamer, 4″h, arched triangular handles.

PLATE 328, MOLD 521. Creamer, 4″h, Covered Sugar, 5″h, pearlized lustre finish.

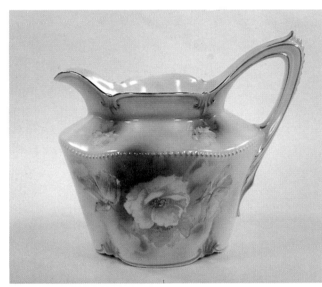

PLATE 329, MOLD 521. Pitcher, 6½″h.

PLATE 330, MOLD 522. "Ribbon and Jewel" Mold, Pitcher, 10″h, Mill scene, jewels undecorated. Unmarked examples also have been seen in this mold. Also see Plate 415 in Vertical Objects and Plates 68, 69, and 70 in Flat Objects.

PLATE 331, MOLD 523. Cups, 3″h, pearlized lustre finish.

PLATE 332, MOLD 524. Mustache Cup, 3″h, 3″d, gold and white enamelling, unmarked, except for raised star, Mark 13.

PLATE 333, MOLD 525. "Stippled Floral" Mold, Coffee Pot, 9″h, Roses. Also see Plates 78 to 81 in Flat Objects and Plates 436 and 437 in Accessory Items.

PLATE 334, MOLD 525. "Stippled Floral" Mold, Tankard, 13"h, Roses.

PLATE 335, MOLD 525. "Stippled Floral" Mold, Tankard, 13"h, Lilies, unmarked.

PLATE 336, MOLD 525. "Stippled Floral" Mold, Chocolate Set, Pot, 9½"h, Cups, (2) 3"h, Roses, unmarked.

PLATE 337, MOLD 525. "Stippled Floral" Mold, Tankard, 14"h, Roses.

133

PLATE 338, MOLD 525. "Stippled Floral" Mold, Creamer, 3½"h, Roses.

PLATE 339, MOLD 525. "Stippled Floral" Mold, Mustard Pot and ladle, 2½"h, Hanging Basket decor.

PLATE 340, MOLD 525. Covered Sugar, 4½"h, Creamer, 3"h, Roses.

PLATE 341, MOLD 526. "Carnation" Mold, Tankard, 11½″, Poppies. Also see Plates 325 and 341 to 351 in Vertical Objects and Plates 4 to 99 in Flat Objects.

PLATE 342, MOLD 526. "Carnation" Mold, Tankard, 12½″h, Roses, unmarked.

PLATE 343, MOLD 526. "Carnation" Mold, Tankard, 12½″h, Roses.

PLATE 344, MOLD 526. "Carnation" Mold, Tankard, 11½″, Roses.

PLATE 345, MOLD 526. "Carnation" Mold, Tankard, 13″h, Poppies, satin finish.

PLATE 346, MOLD 526. "Carnation" Mold, Lemonade Pitcher, 9½" h, watered silk finish.

PLATE 347, MOLD 526. "Carnation" Mold, Chocolate Pot, 10" h, satin finish.

PLATE 348, MOLD 526. "Carnation" Mold, Tankard, 14" h, Sugar, 4" h, Creamer, 4" h, Roses, satin finish.

PLATE 349, MOLD 526. "Carnation" Mold, Syrup Pitcher, 3" h, satin and watered silk finish.

PLATE 350, MOLD 526. "Carnation" Mold, Coffee Set, Pot, 10″h, Cup (5) 2″h pearlized and satin finish, Roses.

PLATE 351, MOLD 526. "Carnation" Mold, Shaving Mug, 3½″h.

PLATE 352, MOLD 527. Gravy, 5″d, 2″h, Underplate, 6½″d, 4 dome shapes on border, pearl finish.

PLATE 353, MOLD 528. Covered Candy Dish, 10″l, 7½″w, curved split handle. See Plates 432 and 433 for same body mold. (See R-8 for mold reproduction.)

Vertical Objects (Elevated Scalloped Bases — Plates 354 to 361)

PLATE 354. MOLD 576. Teapot, 5″ h, Castle scene, pearlized lustre on lid.

PLATE 355, MOLD 576. Covered Sugar, 4½″ h, Creamer, 3″ h, Castle scene.

PLATE 356, MOLD 576. Creamer, 3½″h, Covered Sugar, 4″h, Mill scene on creamer, Cottage scene on sugar.

PLATE 357, MOLD 576. Covered Sugar, 4″h, Creamer, 3½″h, Cottage scene.

PLATE 358, MOLD 577. Covered Sugar, 5½"h, 5½"w, Swans, satin finish.

PLATE 359, MOLD 577. Covered Sugar, 5½"h, 5½"w, Creamer, 4½"h, Swan, satin finish.

PLATE 360, MOLD 577. Tea Set, Pot, 7½"h, Creamer, 5"h, Covered Sugar, 5½"h, satin finish.

PLATE 361, MOLD 578. Covered Sugar, 6½"h, square body mold, handles like preceding Mold 577.

Vertical Objects (Pedestal Foot — Plates 362 to 373)

PLATE 362, MOLD 601. Creamer, 4½"h, Covered Sugar, 6"h, round body mold, matte finish.

PLATE 363, MOLD 602. Sugar, 4"h, Creamer, 4"h, 6 sided pedestal base, pearlized lustre finish.

PLATE 364, MOLD 603. Sugar, 4"h, square pedestal base, unmarked.

PLATE 365, MOLD 603. Covered Sugar, 6"h, Creamer, 4"h, Swans, satin finish, unmarked.

PLATE 366, MOLD 604. Creamer, 4"h, round scalloped pedestal base, pearl finish.

PLATE 367, MOLD 605. Creamer, 4"h, round scalloped pedestal base, gold stencilled designs.

PLATE 368, MOLD 606. Creamer, 4½"h, Covered Sugar, 6"h, reverse scalloped border, Pheasant decor.

PLATE 369, MOLD 607. Covered Sugar, 5"h, Creamer, 3½"h, round scalloped base, looped handles.

PLATE 370, MOLD 607. Covered Sugar, 5"h, Roses, gold stencilled designs.

PLATE 371, MOLD 608. Tea Set, Pot, 5½"h, 7"w, Sugar, 5"h, Creamer, 4"h, designs in relief at base of handles, Roses and Snowballs, gold spattered outer border.

PLATE 372, MOLD 609. "Fleur-de-lys" Mold, Shaving Mug, 3½"h, short pedestal base, pearlized lustre finish, Roses. Also see Plates 46 to 49 in Flat Objects.

PLATE 373, MOLD 609. "Fleur-de-lys" Mold, Tea Set, Pot, 6"h, 8"w, Sugar, 5½"h, Creamer, 4"h, Summer portrait, satin finish.

Vertical Objects (Molded Feet — Plates 374 to 415)

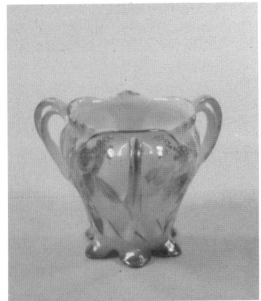

PLATE 374, MOLD 626. "Sunflower" Mold, Covered Sugar, 4½″h, Creamer, 3″h, molded scalloped foot, double twisted handles and finial, pearlized lustre finish. Also see Plate 293 in Vertical Objects and Plates 107 and 108 in Flat Objects.

PLATE 375, MOLD 627. 3 Handled Toothpick Holder, 2½″h, molded petal feet.

PLATE 376, MOLD 627. Demi-tasse Cup, 3″h, Floral decor.

PLATE 377, MOLD 627. Cup, 2½″h, satin finish.

PLATE 378, MOLD 628. "Iris" Mold. Chocolate Pot, 11″h, molded scalloped foot, Fruit decor. Also see Plate 324 in Vertical Objects and Plates 83 to 87 in Flat Objects.

PLATE 379, MOLD 628. "Iris" Mold, Chocolate Pot, 11″h, satin finish, Poppies.

PLATE 380, MOLD 628. "Iris" Mold, Creamer, 4″h, Poppies.

PLATE 381, MOLD 629. Cup, 2½″h, short molded scalloped foot.

PLATE 382, MOLD 630. Chocolate Pot, 10″h, handpainted, Roses, RSP Mark 8.

PLATE 383, MOLD 631. "Medallion" Mold, Syrup Pitcher, 6"h, underplate, 6"d, 4 molded feet, ornate pierced finial, cameo portrait of "Josephine" on gold tapestry bkgrd. Also see Plates 55 to 62 in Flat Objects.

PLATE 384, MOLD 631. Reverse side of preceding Syrup Pitcher, "Napoleon" cameo portrait on gold tapestry bkgrd with Sitting Basket decor.

PLATE 385, MOLD 631. "Medallion" Mold, Syrup Pitcher, 6″h, Reflecting Water Lilies.

PLATE 386, MOLD 631. "Medallion" Mold, Cracker Jar, 6½″h, 8½″w, gold stippled border, Poppies.

PLATE 387, MOLD 632. Covered Sugar, 3″h, Creamer, 3″h, 8 ball shaped molded feet, ball shaped finial, handle varies in this mold by size of object.

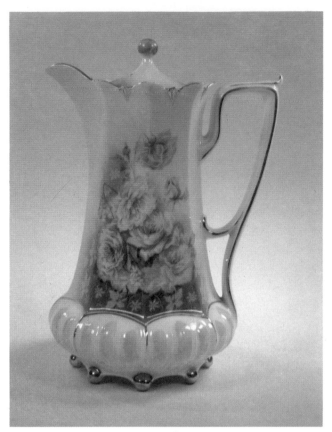

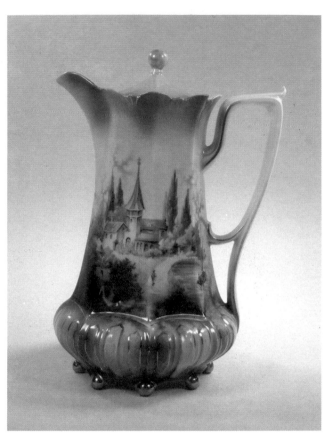

PLATE 388, MOLD 632. Chocolate Pot, 9½"h, note handle differs from preceding object same mold, Plate 387.

PLATE 389, MOLD 632. Chocolate Pot, 9½"h, Castle scene.

PLATE 390, MOLD 632. Chocolate Pot, 9½"h, Poppies.

PLATE 391, MOLD 633. Chocolate Pot, 11"h, 8 molded feet, beaded top border, molded "Laurel" chain undecorated at top, pearlized lustre finish, Turkeys and Birds.

PLATE 392, MOLD 633. Chocolate Set, Pot, 11″h, Cups, 3″h (4), satin finish, Laurel Chain and Hanging Basket decor.

PLATE 393, MOLD 634. Cracker Jar, 6½″h, 8″w, 4 molded feet, pearlized lustre finish, Surreal Dogwood Blossoms.

PLATE 394, MOLD 635. Tea Pot, 7″h, 7″w, pearlized lustre finish, Surreal Dogwood Blossoms, gold enamelling, 4 molded feet.

PLATE 395, MOLD 636. Cracker Jar, 6″h, 8½″w, 4 molded feet, Lilies.

PLATE 396, MOLD 637. Mustache Cup, 2½"h, 4 molded feet, pearlized lustre finish.

PLATE 397, MOLD 638. Creamer, 4"h, 6 molded feet, Spring portrait.

PLATE 398, MOLD 639. Creamer, 4½"h, molded scalloped footed base, Floral decor.

PLATE 399, MOLD 640. Ewer, 5"h, rococo border and handle, Swan scene.

PLATE 400, MOLD 641. "Icicle" Mold, Chocolate Pot, 10″ h, pearl finish, Swans through Evergreens front, Evergreens on back (not shown).
Also see Plates 42 to 45 in Flat Objects.

PLATE 401, MOLD 641. "Icicle" Mold, Sugar, 3½″ h, Barnyard Animals.

PLATE 402, MOLD 641. "Icicle" Mold, Mustard Pot, 4″ h, Reflecting Water Lilies, unmarked.

PLATE 403, MOLD 641. "Icicle" Mold, Toothpick Holder, 2½″ h, Roses and Snowballs.

PLATE 404, MOLD 642. Chocolate Pot, 10½″h, 6 molded feet, 2 part handle with embossed beads, similar finial, beaded border, small "opal" jewel at top, Roses and Snowballs.

PLATE 405, MOLD 642. Chocolate Set, Pot, 12″h, Cup (4) 3″h, jewel undecorated.

PLATE 406, MOLD 643. Coffee Pot, 10″, 6 molded feet in drape fashion, ornate 2 part handle, floral finial, jewels at top, decorated as opals.

PLATE 407, MOLD 643. Covered Sugar, 4″h, 6″w, jewels undecorated.

PLATE 408, MOLD 643. Covered Sugar, 6″h, 8″w, satin finish, jewels undecorated.

PLATE 409, MOLD 643. Coffee Pot, 10″h, jewels undecorated.

PLATE 410, MOLD 643. Cider Pitcher, 6″h, 6″w, Melon Eaters, undecorated jewels, handle variation.

PLATE 411, MOLD 643. Covered Sugar, 6″h, Creamer, 4″h, satin finish, gold stippled designs, jewels decorated as opals.

PLATE 412, MOLD 644. Mustache Cup, 3½″h, molded feet, flared scrolled top, Poppies.

PLATE 413, MOLD 644. Chocolate Pot, 11″h, ring type finial, Floral decor.

PLATE 414, MOLD 644. Covered Sugar, 3½"h, Castle scene, Creamer, 3½"h, Mill scene.

PLATE 415, MOLD 645. Covered Sugar, 5½"h, Creamer, 4"h, 8 molded feet, jewels decorated as opals, Lebrun portrait on gold tapestry bkgrd, jewels on handles painted gold.

Vertical Objects (Applied Feet Plates — 416 to 422)

PLATE 416, MOLD 701. Covered Sugar, 4½″h, Creamer 3½″h, 4 applied feet, ring type finial, Mill scene on Sugar, Castle scene on Creamer.

PLATE 417, MOLD 702. Covered Sugar, 4½″h, Creamer, 3½″h, 4 applied feet, embossed ribbed body, beaded handle, ring type finial, Indian Runner Duck decor.

PLATE 418, MOLD 703. Sugar, 4 applied feet, scalloped top, unmarked.

PLATE 419, MOLD 703. Creamer, 3½″h, gold spattered handle, unmarked.

PLATE 420, MOLD 704. Chocolate Pot, 10″h, 4 applied "fleur-de-lys" shaped feet, beaded and pierced handle, satin finish.

PLATE 421, MOLD 704. Tea Pot, 7″h, 8″w, satin finish, Surreal Dogwood Blossoms.

PLATE 422, MOLD 704. Cup, 2½″h, Laurel Chain pattern.

Accessory Items (Plates 423 to 438)

PLATE 423, MOLD 726. Hatpin Holder, 3 footed, 5"h, Floral decor.

PLATE 424, MOLD 727. Hatpin Holder, 4½"h, four sided scrolled top, Roses.

PLATE 425, MOLD 728. Hatpin Holder, 4½"h, 6 sided mold, House view of Sheepherder I scene. This mold has also been seen with the RSG Mark 25.

PLATE 426, MOLD 728. Hatpin Holder, 4½"h, satin finish, Hanging Basket decor.

PLATE 427, MOLD 729. Hatpin Holder, 4½"h, scalloped crimped top and bottom, satin finish, Roses.

PLATE 428, MOLD 776. Muffineer, 5"h, flared base with molded pierced handles.

PLATE 429, MOLD 777. Muffineer, 4½"h, Roses.

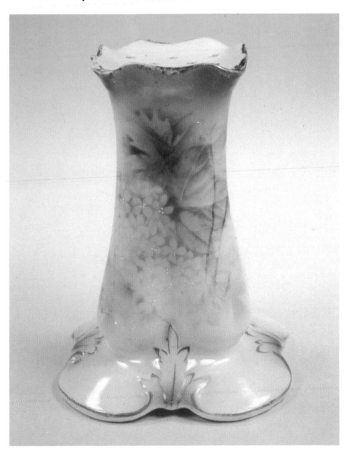

PLATE 430, MOLD 801. Talcum Shaker, 4½"h, scalloped skirted base, Snowballs.

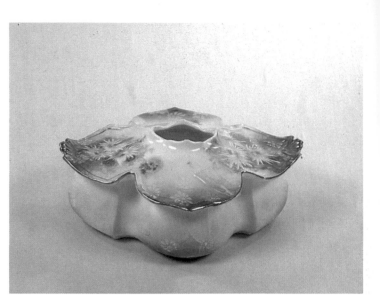

PLATE 431, MOLD 801. Hair Receiver, 2″h, 4½″d, molded feet, gold tapestry work, Roses.

PLATE 432, MOLD 802. Hair Receiver, 2″h, 6″l, 4 sided scalloped base and top, same body mold as Mold 528, Plate 353.

PLATE 433, MOLD 802. Hair Receiver, 2″h, 6″l, gold stencilled designs, RSP Mark 10.

PLATE 434, MOLD 803. Hair Receiver, 5″sq, satin finish.

PLATE 435, MOLD 804. Hair Receiver, 3″h, 5″d, round blown out body, Laurel chain decor.

PLATE 436, MOLD 805. "Stippled Floral" Mold, Hair Receiver, handpainted, artist signed "Kolb," Mark 29. Also see Plates 333 to 340 in Vertical Objects and Plates 78 to 81 in Flat Objects.

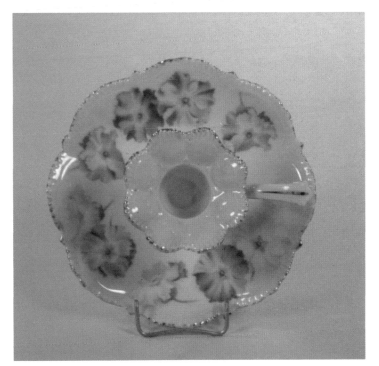

PLATE 437, MOLD 826. "Stippled Floral" Mold, Hairpin Holder, 4½″l, 1½″h, hairpin form on top of lid, satin finish, Récamier portrait, unmarked. Also see Plates 333 to 340 and 436 in Vertical Objects and Plates 78 to 81 in Flat Objects.

PLATE 438, MOLD 851. Chamberstick, 2½″h, 3½″d base, pearl finish.

Ferners and Vases (Plates 439 to 455)

PLATE 439, MOLD 876. Ferner, 3½"h, 7"w, scalloped top, blown out base, unmarked pieces have been seen in this mold, see Plates 301 to 303.

PLATE 440, MOLD 877. Ferner, 7"h, 6"d, 8 sided, satin finish.

PLATE 441, MOLD 878. Ferner, 3½"h, 8½"d, scalloped border, molded feet, Swans and Terrace scene.

PLATE 442, MOLD 878. Ferner, 3½"h, 8½"d, Mill scene.

PLATE 443, MOLD 900. Vase, 9″h, pear shaped body, scalloped molded foot, art nouveau type handles, hand-painted, enamelling on Roses, RSP Mark 9.

PLATF 444, MOLD 900. Vase, 11"h, Autumn portrait, gold stippled work.

PLATE 445, MOLD 900. Ewer, 6½"h, Autumn portrait, cobalt top and bottom.

PLATE 446, MOLD 901. Vase, 8½"h, blown out puffed pinched neck, beaded pierced handles, undecorated tear drop jewel, Bird of Paradise.

PLATE 447, MOLD 902. Vase, 12"h, pedestal foot, rococo handles, Pheasant decor.

PLATE 448, MOLD 903. Covered Urn, 12½"h, Cottage scene.

PLATE 449, MOLD 903. Covered Urn, 12½"h, pedestal foot, blown out and pointed finial, Mill scene.

PLATE 450, MOLD 904. Vase, 10½″ h, flared top, pedestal base, curved scroll type handles, satin finish on body, iridescent Tiffany finish on base.

PLATE 451, MOLD 905. Vase, 9″ h, flared neck, scalloped molded foot, reverse curved handles.

PLATE 452, MOLD 906. Vase, 11″h, short neck with tapering cone shaped body, Sheepherder II scene.

PLATE 453, MOLD 907. Vase, 3½″h, Mill scene.

PLATE 454, MOLD 908. Vase, 6½″h, pear shaped body, ornate designs in relief applied to each side, Man in the Mountain scene.

PLATE 455, MOLD 909. Vase, 5″h, short neck, full body, Cottage scene.

Other Suhl and Tillowitz Photographs

PLATE 456. Bowl, 11½"l, 11"w, molded handle, Harvest decor, cobalt to flow blue coloring, Mark 2.

PLATE 457. Bowl, 10"d, Greek Key and gold stencilled designs, molded flowers, unmarked.

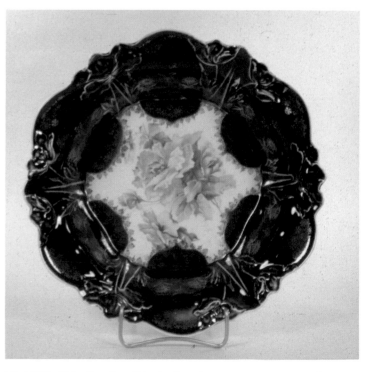

PLATE 458. Bowl, 10"d, 6 dome shapes with 3 decorated, Mark 1.

PLATE 459. Bowl, 10½"d, floral center, black bkgrd, same mold as Plates 477 and 478, unmarked.

PLATE 460. Bowl, 10½"d, pearlized lustre finish, unmarked except for Mold Mark 14.

PLATE 461. Bowl, 9½"d, Lilacs, Mark 1.

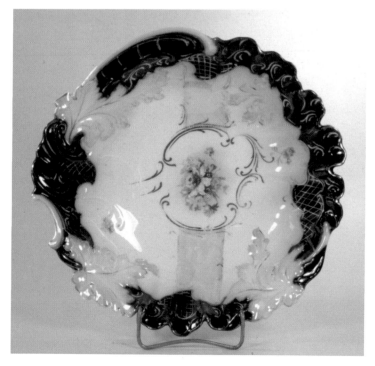

PLATE 462. Bowl, 10½"d, "Keyhole" center, Mark 1.

PLATE 463. Bowl, 9½"d, molded floral shapes, iridescent border, unmarked.

PLATE 464. Vase, 6"h, Mark 1.

PLATE 465. Cup, 2½"h, Saucer, 5½"d, part of set, Mark 1.

PLATE 466. Tea Set, Pot, 6½"h, Creamer, 4"h, Sugar, 5"h, Mark 1.

PLATE 467. Cracker Jar, 6"h, 5"w, Mark 14.

PLATE 468. Covered Butter Dish, 6″h, 7″d. Underplate is same mold as RSP Mold 343 (Plates 258 to 261). Mark 3, also seen unmarked.

PLATE 469. Cake Plate, 10″d, heavy gold border, same mold as RSP Mold 343, Mark 3.

PLATE 470. Dessert Set, Cake Plate, 10″d, individual bowls, 5½″d, cameo women figurals on border of Cake Plate, Cupids on small bowls, iridescent finish, unmarked. Same mold as RSP Mold 343 and preceding Plate 468, Mark 3.

PLATE 471. Nappy, satin finish border, enamelling on flowers, Mark 1.

PLATE 472. Ladies' Spittoon, 2"h, 4"d, Flow Blue Coloring, Mark 2.

PLATE 473. Cracker Jar, 5½"h, 8½"d, double handles, Mark 3.

PLATE 474. Plate, 10″d, pierced on sides, enamelling on flowers, Mark 3.

PLATE 475. Bowl, 10½″d, satin finish inside border, Mark 3.

PLATE 476. Bowl, 7½″l, 4½″w, Mark 1.

PLATE 477. Bowl, 10″d, blown out sides with molded floral shapes, unmarked.

PLATE 478. Bowl, 10″d, Victorian Lady with Dog, bronze iridescent Tiffany finish, same mold as Plate 477 and 459. This particular mold may be unmarked, or have Steeple Mark 1 or 3, or RSP Mark 4.

PLATE 479. Vase, 11″h, art nouveau shape, portrait decor, turquoise tapestry finish, Mark 20.

PLATE 480. Pitcher. 5½″h, Parrots, unmarked or R. S. Suhl Mark 16.

PLATE 481. Vase, 10″h, "Lady with Peacock," turquoise tapestry finish, Mark 20.

PLATE 482. Reverse side of Plate 481, "Lady with Doves," turquoise tapestry finish.

PLATE 483. Plate, 8½″d, Gibson Girl portrait, Mark 20.

PLATE 484. Plate, 8½″d, Gibson Girl portrait, Mark 20.

PLATE 485. Plate, 8½″d, Gibson Girl portrait, Mark 20.

PLATE 486. Plate, 8½″d, Gibson Girl portrait, Mark 20.

PLATE 487. Bowl, 10½"d, scrolled border mold, 6 sided recessed center, satin finish, variation of Mark 23 in red (crown only) in raised circle mold mark.

PLATE 488. Bowl, 10"d, pierced border, gold lustre on border, Mark 23.

PLATE 489. Bowl, 6"d, Fruit decor, Mark 20.

PLATE 490. Cake Plate, Roses, Mark 20.

PLATE 491. Tea Strainer, 6"l, Mark 18.

PLATE 492. Cup, 2"h, 3½"d, Saucer, 5½"d, Mark 20.

PLATE 493. Plate, 8½"d, handpainted, Mark 21.

PLATE 494. Toothbrush Holder, 4"l, Mark 20.

PLATE 495. Vase, 11½″h, art nouveau shape, "Lady with Peacock," gold stippled frame, pearl lustre finish, Mark 23.

PLATE 496. Plate, 8″d, portrait decor, gold stippled designs, Mark 19.

PLATE 497. Vase, 11″h, rococo shape, Figural decor, Mark 22.

PLATE 498. Cake Plate, 10″d, rococo border, "Lady with Doves," gold stippled frame, turquoise tapestry designs, gold enamelling, Mark 23.

PLATE 499. Cup, 5″h, pedestal base, Figural decor, gold stencilled designs, Mark 20.

PLATE 500. Bowl, 6″d, Classical scene after Kauffman (note name at bottom), Mark 16.

PLATE 501. Plate, 8½″d, Windmill and water scene, Mark 20.

PLATE 502. Shell (Variation of RSP Shell Mold 20), pearl lustre finish, Mark 25 with "Germany" incised.

PLATE 503. Creamer, 3″h, Sugar, 3″h (RSP Mold 505, Plate 306), pearl lustre finish, Mark 25.

PLATE 504. Bun Tray, 14″l, 6½″w, (RSP Mold 207, Plate 192), Sitting Basket decor, Mark 26.

189

PLATE 505. Plate, 8″d, Tulips, handpainted, matte finish, Mark 25 with gold script "Handpainted."

PLATE 506. Compote, 3″h, 7″d, Tulips, handpainted, Mark 25 with gold script "Handpainted."

PLATE 507. Bowl, 9½″d, Tulips, Mark 25 with gold script "Handpainted."

PLATE 508. Plate, 8″d, floral decor, handpainted, artist signed "Pavec," Mark 28.

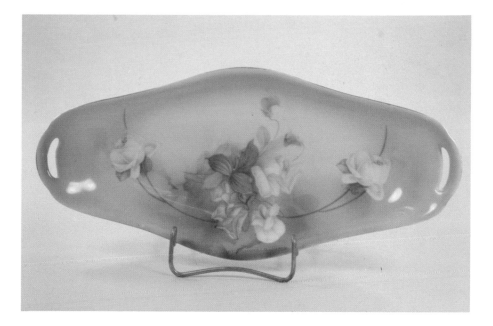

PLATE 509. Celery, 12½"l, floral decor, handpainted, Marks 27 and 29.

PLATE 510. Plate, 8"d, Tulips, handpainted, Mark 29.

PLATE 511. Berry Set, Master Bowl, 10"d, individual bowls, 5"d (8), floral decor, handpainted, artist signed "Wallet," Mark 28.

PLATE 512. Plate, 9″d, Calla Lilies, Mark 25.

PLATE 513. Bowl, 10″d, Snowballs, Mark 24.

PLATE 514. Plate, 7″d, Tulips, Mark 25.

PLATE 515. Relish, 8½″l, 4″w, art nouveau decor, matte finish, Mark 25.

PLATE 516. Bread Tray, 11″l, 7″w, Mark 24.

PLATE 517. Relish, 8½″l, 4″w, Mark 27.

PLATE 518. Relish, 7½″l, 4″w, Mark 25.

PLATE 519. Bowl, 7½"l, 6"w, pierced sides, pearlized lustre finish, Mill scene (note scene is different from RSP mill scene), Mark 25.

PLATE 520. Bowl, 7"l, 5½"w, Game Birds, Mark 25.

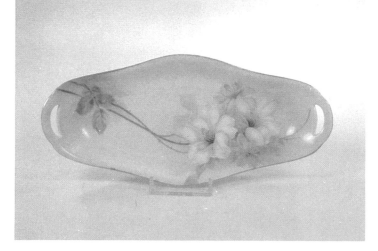

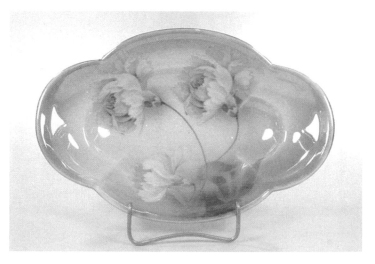

PLATE 521. Relish, 9"l, 4"w, Mark 27.

PLATE 522. Bowl, 10"l, 6½"w, pierced sides, pearl lustre finish.

PLATE 523. Plate, 6½"d, Roses, Mark 25.

PLATE 524. Bowl, 6"d, Tulips, Mark 25.

PLATE 525. Bowl, 9½"d, Floral decor, Mark 25.

PLATE 526. Plate, 6"d, Stylized Floral decor, Mark 27.

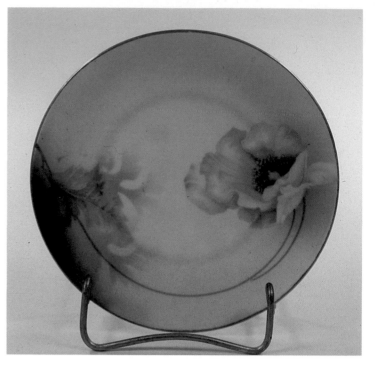

PLATE 527. Bowl, 5″d, pearl lustre finish, Mark 27.

PLATE 528. Plate 6″d, Poppy, Mark 27.

PLATE 529. Plate, 8½″d, Daffodils, Mark 25.

PLATE 530. Bowl, 5″d, Floral decor, Mark 27.

PLATE 531. Footed Bowl, 3″h, 7½″d, Floral decor, Mark 27.

PLATE 532. Bowl, 5″d, Floral decor, Mark 25.

PLATE 533. Plate, 6½″d, Floral decor, Mark 25.

PLATE 534. Plate, 6″d, pearl lustre finish, same mold as RSP Mold 202, (Plate 181), Mark 25 with "Germany" incised.

PLATE 535. Chocolate Pot, Art Deco mold, Mark 27.

PLATE 536. Plate, 10″, pierced sides, "Man with Horses," Mark 25.

PLATE 537. Bowl, 9″ sq., Art Deco mold, Sheepherder scene, Mark 27.

PLATE 538. Chocolate Pot, Art Deco mold, Cottage scene (different from cottage scene on RSP objects), Mark 27.

PLATE 539. Talcum Shaker, 4″ h, pearl finish, gold enamelling, Mark 25.

PLATE 540. Pitcher, 6½″ h, 10″ w, four footed, Mark 27.

PLATE 541. Talcum Shaker, 4½"h, molded scalloped base, pearl finish, Mark 25.

PLATE 542. Hatpin Holder, 4½"h, Reflecting Water Lilies, Mark 27.

PLATE 543. Hatpin Holder, 4½"h, Poppies, Mark 27.

PLATE 544. Muffineer, 4½"h, (see RSP Mold 777), Mark 25.

PLATE 545. Hair Receiver, 2″h, 4″d, handpainted blank, Mark 25.

PLATE 546. 3 Handled Toothpick Holder, handpainted blank, Mark 25.

PLATE 547. Creamer, 4″h, handpainted blank, artist signed, Mark 25.

PLATE 548. Inkwell, 3″h, 3″d, handpainted blank, artist signed on back, Mark 25.

PLATE 549. Vase, 6″h, handpainted blank, Mark 25.

PLATE 550. Bowl, 7½″d, four pierced sides, handpainted blank, Game Bird, artist signed, Mark 25 with a black palette artist's mark.

PLATE 551. Tea Tile, 6″d, high lustre glaze, Mark 25.

PLATE 552. Wall Pocket Vase, 9″l, Parrot, undecorated blank, Mark 27.

PLATE 553. Jam Jar, 4½"h, Mark 25.

PLATE 554. Demi-Tasse Cup, 3"h, Saucer, 4½"d, satin finish, gold stencilled designs, Mark 25.

PLATE 555. Covered Sugar, 3"h, 6"w, Roses, Mark 24.

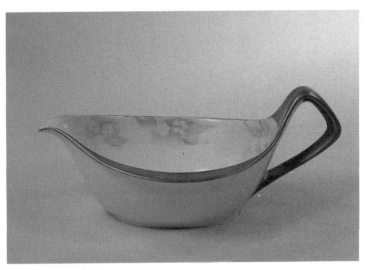

PLATE 556. Sauce Dish, 6"l, handpainted blank, Mark 25.

PLATE 557. Footed Bowl, 3"h, 6"d, Mark 27.

PLATE 558. Pin Box, 2"h, Poppy, Mark 27.

PLATE 559. Footed Bowl, 2½"h, 6"d, pierced handles, hand-painted, Mark 25 with gold script "Handpainted," and artist mark "M. W. C." in gold.

PLATE 560. Egg Cup, 3½"h, inside liner, "Cottonplant" decor, Mark 25 with "Cottonplant" pattern mark in red.

PLATE 561. Demi-Tasse, Cup, 2"h, Saucer, 4½"d, scalloped feet, Roses, Mark 27.

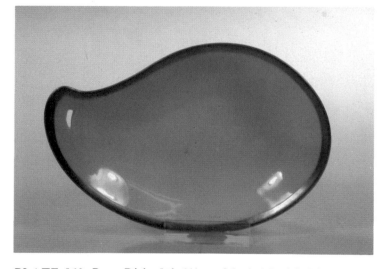

PLATE 562. Bone Dish, 5"l, 3½"w, Mark 25 with "Germany" incised.

PLATE 563. Cup, 2"h, 3½"d, Roses, Mark 25.

PLATE 564. Tray, 15½"l, 5"w, Mark 31 in blue.

PLATE 565. Place Setting from Dinner Service, Mark 31.

PLATE 566. Berry Set, Master Bowl, 10″d, Individual Bowls, 5″d, Roses, Mark 30 (without handpainted).

PLATE 567. Creamer, 2″h, Covered Sugar, 2½″h, Floral decor, Mark 30 (without handpainted).

PLATE 568. Bowl, 6″l, 5″w, Roses, Mark 24.

PLATE 569. Bowl, pierced sides, gold stencilled designs, Lilies, handpainted, Mark 30.

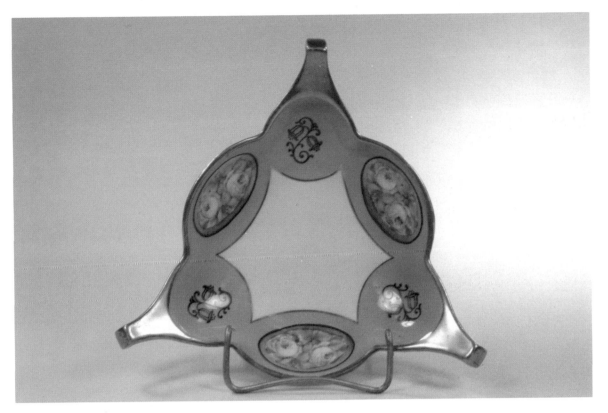

PLATE 570. Bowl, Art Deco Triangular shape, 7″l, Mark 30.

PLATE 571. Bowl, 2″h, 6″d, White Florals on black bkgrd, Mark 30.

PLATE 572. Covered Sugar, 2½″h, 4″d, Mark 33.

PLATE 573. Plate, 6½″d, Floral decor, Mark 34.

PLATE 574. Jardiniere, footed, 7″h, 6½″w, Tulips, Mark 34.

PLATE 575. Vase, 9″h, Floral decor, gold stencilled designs,
Mark 27. This mold is seen with various R. S. marks.

PLATE 576. Pair of Vases, Roses, 12½″h, Mark 34.

Misleading Marks and Objects

PLATE R1. Reproduced R. S. Prussia Mark.

PLATE R2. in red, initials, wreath, and star.

PLATE R3. in red, initials, wreath, and star.

PLATE R4. wreath and star.

PLATE R5. Salt and Pepper, 2½"h, Roses, Mark R1.

PLATE R6. Egg, Figural decor, 5½"l, "signed" Boucher, Mark R4.

PLATE R7. Cracker Jar, 8″h, Roses, Mark R2.

PLATE R9. Ewer, 5″h. See RSP Mold 640, Plate 399.

PLATE R8. Candy Dish, 8″l, 6″w, Mark R4. See RSP Mold 528, Plate 353.

PLATE R10. Jewel Box, 10″l, 8″w, "signed" Boucher, Mark R2.

PLATE R11. Plate, 7″d, "signed" Boucher, Mark R3.

PLATE R12. Shoe, Mark R3.

PLATE R13. Saucer (from set), 5½"d, Mark R3.

PLATE R14. Hatpin Holder, 5½"h, Mark R3.

PLATE R15. Cracker Jar, 7"h, Mark R1.

PLATE 16. Cracker Jar, 5"h, Mark R1.

PLATE R17. Mustache Cup, 3½"h, Mark R1.

BIBLIOGRAPHY

Ananoff, Alexandre. *L'oeuvre Dessiné de François Boucher.* Paris: F. De Nobele, Librarie, 1966.

Barber, Edwin Atlee. *The Ceramic Collectors' Glossary.* New York: Da Capo Press, 1967.

Barlock, George E. and Eileen. *The Treasures of R. S. Prussia,* 1976.

Bartran, Margaret. *A Guide to Color Reproductions.* Second edition. Metuchen, New Jersey: The Scarecrow Press, Inc., 1971.

Bearne, Mrs. *A Court Painter and His Circle, François Boucher.* London: Adelphi Terrace, 1913.

Benson, E. F. *The White Eagle of Poland.* New York: George H. Doran Company, n. d.

Boger, Louise Ade. *The Dictionary of World Pottery and Porcelain.* New York: Charles Scribner's Sons, 1971.

Buell, Raymond Leslie. *Poland: Key to Europe.* London: Jonathan Cape, 1939.

Calvert, Albert F. (ed.). Murillo. *The Spanish Series.* London: John Lane, The Bodley Head Gallery, MCMVII.

Castries, Duc de. *Madame Récamier.* Hachette, 1971.

Catalogue of Reproductions of Paintings Prior to 1860. Paris: Unesco, 1972.

Chaffers, William. *Handbook of Marks and Monograms on Pottery and Porcelain.* Revised edition. London: William Reeves, 1968.

_____. *Marks & Monograms on Pottery and Porcelain.* Vol. 1, 15th Revised edition. London: William Reeves, 1965.

Chróscicki, Leon. *Porcelana — Znaki Wytworni Europejskich.* Warszawa: Wybawnictwo Artystyczno-Graficzne, 1974.

Cox, W. E. *The Book of Pottery and Porcelain.* Vol. 1. New York: L. Lee Shepard Co., Inc., 1944.

Cushion, J. P. *Pocket Book of German Ceramic Marks and Those of Other Central European Countries.* London: Faber and Faber, 1961.

Cushion, J. P. (in collaboration with W. B. Honey). *Handbook of Pottery and Porcelain Marks.* London: Faber & Faber, 1956.

Danckert, Ludwig. *Handbuch des Europäischen Porzellans.* Muncher: Prestel-Verlag, 1954.

Day, William E. *Blue Book of Art Values.* Third edition. Paducah, Kentucky: Collector Books, 1979.

Dyboski, Roman. *Outlines of Polish History.* London: George Allen & Unwin, Ltd. Revised edition, 1931.

Encyclopedia Britannica, Inc. Vol. 18. Chicago: William Benton, 1970.

Fayard, Arthème (Ed.). *Souvenirs De Mme. Louise Elisabeth Vigée-Le Brun.* Paris: F. Funch-Bretana.

Gaston, Mary Frank. *The Collector's Encyclopedia of Limoges Porcelain.* Paducah, Kentucky: Collector Books, 1980.

Graul, Richard and Albrecht Kurzwelly. *Alt Thuringer Porzellan,* 1909.

Haggar, Reginald G. *The Concise Encyclopedia of Continental Pottery and Porcelain.* New York: Hawthorne Books, Inc., 1960.

Hall, James. *Dictionary of Subjects and Symbols in Art.* Revised edition. New York: Harper & Row, 1979.

Hammond, Dorothy. *Confusing Collectibles.* Des Moines, Iowa: Wallace Homestead, 1969.

Honey, W. B. *German Porcelain.* London: Faber and Faber, MCMXLVII.

Hyamson, Albert M. *A Dictionary of Universal Biography of all Ages and of all People.* Second edition. New York: E. P. Dutton & Co., Inc., 1951.

LaRousse Encyclopedia of World Geography. New York: Odyssey Press. Adapted from *Geographie Universelle Larousse.* Western Publishing Co., 1965.

Leistikow-Duchardt, Annelore. *Die Entwicklung eines neuen Stiles im Porzellan.* Heidelberg: Carl Winter Universitatsverlag, 1957.

Lewis, C. T. Courtney. *The Picture Printer of the Nineteenth Century: George Baxter.* London: Sampson Low, Marsten & Co., Ltd., 1911.

Lucas, E. V. *Chardin and Vigée-Lebrun.* London: Methuen & Co., Ltd., n. d.

Meyers Grosses Konversations-Lexikon. 6th ed. Vol. 17. Leipzig and Vienna: Bibliographisches Institut, 1907.

Mountfield, David. *The Antique Collectors' Illustrated Dictionary.* London: Hamlyn, 1974.

Muehsam, Gerd (ed.). *French Painters and Paintings from the Fourteenth Century to Post Impressionism.* New York: Frederich Ungar Publishing Co., 1970.

Norman, Geraldine. *Nineteenth-Century Painters and Painting: A Dictionary.* Thames and Hudson, 1977.

Penkala, Maria. *European Porcelain A Handbook for the Collector.* Second edition. Rutland, Vermont: Charles E. Tuttle, 1968.

Poche, Emanuel. *Porcelain Marks of the World.* New York: Arco Publishing Co., Inc., 1974.

Rose, William John. *The Drama of Upper Silesia.* Brattleboro, Vermont: Stephen Daye Press, 1935.

Schlegelmilch, Clifford J. *Handbook of Erdmann and Reinhold Schlegelmilch, Prussia-Germany and Oscar Schlegelmilch, Germany.* Third edition, 1973.

Sorenson, Don C. *My Collection R. S. Prussia,* 1979.

Stryienski, Casimir (ed.). *Memoirs of the Countess Potocka.* New York: Doubleday & McClure Co., 1901.

Thalheim, Karl G. and A. Hillen Ziegfeld (eds.). *Der deutsche Osten. Seine Geschichte, sein Wesen und seine Aufgabe.* Berlin: Propylaen, 1936.

The Antique Trader Price Guide to Antiques. Dubuque, Iowa: Babka Publishing Company, Inc., Summer 1979, Volume X, No. 2, Issue No. 32.

The Ceramist. Vol. 3. Winter Quarter, 1923.

The International Geographic Encyclopedia and Atlas. Boston: Houghton Mifflin Company, 1979.

The World Book Atlas. Field Enterprises Educational Corporation, 1973.

Thorne, J. O. (ed). *Chambers Biographical Dictionary.* Revised edition. New York: St. Martin's Press, 1969.

Treharne, R. F. and Harold Fullard (eds.). *Muir's Historical Atlas Medieval and Modern.* Tenth edition. New York: Barnes and Noble, Inc., 1964.

Wandycz, Piotr S. *The Lands of Partitioned Poland, 1795-1918.* Seattle: University of Washington Press, 1923.

Webster's Biographical Dictionary. Springfield, Mass.: G. and C. Merriam Company, 1976.

Webster's New Geographical Dictionary. Springfield, Mass.; G. and C. Merriam Company, 1972.

Weis, Gustav. *Ullstein Porzellanbuch.* Frankfurt, Berlin, Wein: Verlag Ullstein Gimblt, 1975. First edition, 1964.

Index To Objects

Index To Decoration Themes (RSP Items)

Index To Decoration Themes (Other R. S. and E. S. Marks)

Two Important Tools For The
Astute Antique Dealer, Collector and Investor

Schroeder's Antiques Price Guide

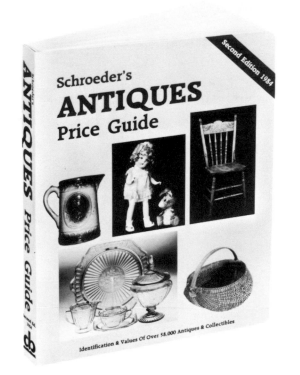

The very best low cost investment that you can make if you are really serious about antiques and collectibles is a good identification and price guide. We publish and highly recommend **Schroeder's Antiques Price Guide.** Our editors and writers are very careful to seek out and report accurate values each year. We do not simply change the values of the items each year but start anew to bring you an entirely new edition. If there are repeats, they are by chance and not by choice. Each huge edition (it weighs 3 pounds!) has over 56,000 descriptions and current values on 608 - 8½x11 pages. There are hundreds and hundreds of categories and even more illustrations. Each topic is introduced by an interesting discussion that is an education in itself. Again, no dealer, collector or investor can afford not to own this book. It is available from your favorite bookseller or antiques dealer at the low price of $9.95. If you are unable to find this price guide in your area, it's available from Collector Books, P. O. Box 3009, Paducah, KY 42001 at $9.95 plus $1.00 for postage and handling.

Schroeder's INSIDER and Price Update

A monthly newsletter published for the antiques and collectibles marketplace.

The **"INSIDER"**, as our subscribers have fondly dubbed it, is a monthly newsletter published for the antiques and collectibles marketplace. It gives the readers timely information as to trends, price changes, new finds, and market moves both upward and downward. Our writers are made up of a panel of well-known experts in the fields of Glass, Pottery, Dolls, Furniture, Jewelry, Country, Primitives, Oriental and a host of other fields in our huge industry. Our subscribers have that "inside edge" that makes them more profitable. Each month we explore 8-10 subjects that are "in", and close each discussion with a random sampling of current values that are recorded at press time. Thousands of subscribers eagerly await each monthly issue of this timely 16-page newsletter. A sample copy is available for $3.00 postpaid. Subscriptions are $24.00 for 12 months; 24 months for $45.00; 36 months for $65.00, all postpaid. A sturdy 3-ring binder to store your **Insider** is available for $5.00 postpaid. This newsletter contains NO paid advertising and is not available on your newsstand. It may be ordered by sending your check or money order to Collector Books, P. O. Box 3009, Paducah, KY 42001.

216